BUSINESS
EVOLVES,
LEADERSHIP
ENDURES

BUSINESS EVOLVES, LEADERSHIP ENDURES

Leadership Traits That Stand the Test of Time

PART OF THE RUSSELL REYNOLDS ASSOCIATES LEADERSHIP SERIES

ANDREA REDMOND
CHARLES TRIBBETT III
BRUCE KASANOFF

EASTON STUDIO PRESS

TEXT DESIGN BY Nan Jerngain
JACKET DESIGN BY Beck Stvan and Nan Jernigan
EDITED BY Amy Handy

Published by Easton Studio Press
P.O. Box 3131
Westport, CT 06880

ISBN 0-97438-06052495
Printed and bound in the United States of America
10 9 8 7 6 5 4 3 2 1

Table of Contents

ACKNOWLEDGMENTS

This effort has first and foremost been a team effort, straight out of Chapter 5, "Team Building." *Business Evolves, Leadership Endures* would not have been possible without the support and help of our firm, Russell Reynolds Associates. Much of the context we provide outside the interviews and historical examples has developed over the years through many discussions with our colleagues on what good leadership looks like and what kind of leader a certain situation requires. So first of all, many, many thanks to all the associates of Russell Reynolds Associates.

We had the pleasure of speaking directly with twenty-six of the world's best leaders, many of whom we have had the honor of knowing personally for many years. We thank them for sharing their time with us so generously and for providing us with the leadership stories that inspired us to write this book. Their illuminating examples have made their enduring leadership traits accessible to all readers to understand and perhaps emulate. Our deepest gratitude goes to Vaughn Beals, Arthur Blank, Taddy Blecher, Marc Breslawsky, Jim Cantalupo, Henri de Castries, Jamie Dimon, Pattie Dunn, Jay Fishman, William Foote, Robert Johnson, Klaus Kleinfeld, Harry Kraemer, Shelly Lazarus, Lord Peter Levene, John A. Luke Jr., Mike McGavick, Rick Menell, Nandan Nilekani, John Pepper, Dave Pottruck, John W. Rogers Jr., Sam Scott, Paul Tagliabue, David Thomas, and William Wrigley Jr.

We would not have been able to write this book without our clients, who are the reason we have the opportunity to work with so many outstanding examples of leadership.

While we owe our entire firm gratitude, some members deserve special recognition. We would like to thank Joseph Bailey III, Henry de Montebello,

Patrick Delhougne, Simon Hearn, and Susanne Lyons for working with us to set up and interview some of the leaders featured in this book. Likewise, the input from our Executive Assessment team has been invaluable. Thank you in particular to Dean Stamoulis and Amy Gershenoff.

The Russell Reynolds Associates Marketing and Communications team, led by Charlotte Rush, was key in making this book a reality. Thank you, Charlotte, for pushing to make this book happen; Matt Hepler, for tireless research and editing; Alyson Nolan, for managing the overall project; and Jane Pook, for support in arranging the interviews.

In addition, we would like to thank Lindsay Levin, of Leader's Quest, for introducing us to some of the world's less known but most inspiring leaders. We would also like to recognize the tremendous efforts of Cubitt Jacobs and Prosek's Amy Airasian, Brian Davis, Carrie Kalish, Mark Kollar, and Jennifer Prosek. The book would not have been published if it were not for the folks at Easton Studio Press, including Nan Jernigan (book design and production), Beck Stvan (jacket design), Amy Handy (editor), Lee Quarfoot (editing and proofreading), and David Wilk at CDS for guidance and support.

We want to recognize Jim Cantalupo in particular. On the day this book was due to our publisher, we learned of Jim's death from a sudden heart attack. Ironically, we feature Jim in our chapter on heart, because he had such great heart for his company, its people, and his job. We hope that his family and colleagues take some comfort in knowing that Jim's brand of leadership embodies what we mean by enduring leadership—the impact of what he accomplished and the spirit in which he brought about those accomplishments will endure for the years to come.

And last, but certainly not least, we wish to thank our families and friends, who lovingly and patiently tolerate the long hours and frequent travel this business requires.

ANDREA REDMOND
CHARLES A. TRIBBETT III

Introduction

What does it take to be a leader in today's business environment? As executive recruiters focused on CEO, board, and other senior executive level positions, we and our colleagues are asked this question over and over again. It is not a recent phenomenon, since our business has always been about finding the right leader for each unique assignment we undertake. However, the rapid rise and fall of the New Economy, accounting scandals and corporate failures, the profound shift in industrial and service jobs from the West to the East, and the near-universal globalization of all business seem to have elevated the debate about leadership. Again and again the media asks if we need new paradigms or models for business leaders today and in the future.

Leaders come with varied styles and backgrounds. Some lead by sheer force of presence, others by a quiet confidence that earns unconditional trust. Some lead by motivation, others by behaviors that set higher standards for all around them. One leader may gain followers through wisdom, another through exceptional credibility earned by hard experience.

Yet there are some universal similarities. Most successful leaders carry within them an unwavering commitment to make a difference, a commitment shaped by a clear conviction or vision. Their personal traits—such as a command of language, a remarkable work ethic, a keen insight and awareness of others. or the fortitude to withstand disappointment—contribute to the essence of leadership; that is, to inspire and lead others to achieve remarkable things.

However, traits alone do not make a leader. Seeing opportunity and seizing that opportunity at the right time and in the right manner are the variables that determine when greatness is realized. Business is never static. Economies ebb and flow, creativity and ingenuity produce new markets almost overnight, and an incident in one country ignites reactions around the world. Having real vision—being able to see around the corners—enables certain leaders to create a new reality that comes as no surprise to them.

Since we are in the business of finding leaders, we have found it useful in these turbulent times to look back upon other eras—where greatness is now widely recognized—and inspect the leadership traits that made inspirational leaders great. Historical leaders hail largely from monarchies, parliaments, the military and religious institutions, with the occasional merchant or explorer thrown in. Beginning with the industrial revolution, the business leader began to occupy a greater share of the leadership stage. In the twentieth century, particularly in the second half, the leadership dialogue switched largely to the business leader. What were the similarities among all these leaders during all these centuries?

You have probably guessed our conclusion. As the title of the book implies, the ingredients of successful leadership endure. In other words, leadership today does not require a brand new model. Rather, we need to spend more time developing the traits and behaviors that have withstood the test of time and have proven over and over again to be effective in motivating large numbers of people to accomplish great things.

This last statement also exposes our answer to the next logical question: Can leadership and these traits be learned or are they predetermined at birth? While certain gifts and talents are indeed a function of DNA, everyone who has a deep commitment to take people to a better place can develop his or her innate skills to be a more effective leader.

We have written this book to help those who are looking for leaders, those who are leaders and want to improve, or those who want to become leaders. Believing that true leadership is all about the person, we have used components of the body (vision, voice, heart, backbone, listening) and the human condition (commitment, team building, emotional intelligence, diversity) to describe what we feel are the enduring traits of leadership.

There are no new management theories in this book; there are no groundbreaking revelations. The world does not need yet another theory on leadership. Instead we offer a back-to-basics reminder of what we do know about leadership: that effective leaders always exhibit one or more of the nine leadership traits we address in this book.

We sought out some obvious and not so obvious leaders in our network and we feature them throughout this book as they tell, in their own words, how they came to recognize a particular leadership trait they possess and how they have used it effectively.

For example, you will see how Dave Pottruck, CEO of Charles Schwab & Co., Inc.—always an intelligent and formidable man—learned how to be more aware of the way others perceive him and to improve both his communication and his listening skills. Or how Klaus Kleinfeld, member of the Executive Committee at Siemens AG, made jokes about his accent in order to remove the biases his coworkers had toward him. .

We have concentrated on corporate leaders but also feature an array of people from other disciplines to make the point that leadership is leadership wherever you find it. We have much to learn from those leaders who occupy not a corner office, but a corner of our hearts.

Leadership is a journey, not a destination. It requires giving rather than taking, and calls for an incredible amount of self-awareness. The returns, however, are many. Having had the privilege of working with so many capable leaders, we wanted to be able to contribute some of that learning to the leadership dialogue in the hope that our readers will find something in this book that will enable them to advance along their own leadership journeys.

1

The Commitment Not to Lead a Little Life

It is better to go down on the great seas
which human hearts were made to sail
than to rot at the wharves in ignoble anchorage.
—Hamilton Wright Mabie[1]

Only those who will risk going too far
can possibly find out how far one can go.
—T. S. Eliot[2]

IF THERE IS ONE TRAIT that all leaders share it is an unshakable conviction to lead a life that matters.

This conviction gives them the courage to challenge the status quo and the determination to keep plowing forward no matter what obstacles they may encounter.

Such admirable strength is contagious and it often motivates others to follow suit and contribute their own best efforts.

Look at any gathering of people—at work, school, legislative sessions, or community meetings—and it soon becomes apparent who *wants* to be in charge, and who is *worthy* of leading. As we all know, these two characteristics are not always found together in the same individual.

We believe the first critical trait of effective leaders—demonstrated repeatedly throughout human history—is an absolute commitment to lead others and institutions to a better place. This commitment to lead a life that matters—a life that counts, rather than a "little life"—is what separates those who merely enjoy authority from those whom others trust, even encourage, to shoulder responsibility.

In almost every case of effective leadership, we find people who believe in a cause or goal with passionate, relentless dedication and are able to rally others to believe in it as well. This commitment is the first step toward enduring leadership—leadership that takes people and organizations to a better place.

•　　•　　•

As a teenager, Sakichi Toyoda dedicated himself to living a very large life. He resolved that he would invent something that would encourage the economic development of nineteenth-century Japan. Familiar with the loom, he began to formulate ways in which it could be made easier to operate, reducing the costs associated with the production of cotton goods. This objective consumed Toyoda, earning him his family's displeasure and leading others to think him an eccentric. But the opinions of others or his own initial failures did not dissuade the young man.

Toyoda continually made improvements to his loom designs. The growing efficiency and improved results of his products attracted the attention of some of Japan's largest trading and spinning companies, which approached him with partnership opportunities. Ultimately, it was with his own businesses, most notably Toyoda Automatic Weaving, where Toyoda saw his greatest successes.

Working with his son, Kiichiro, in 1925 he designed an automatic loom that was capable of being mass-produced. Called the G-type, it was the culmination of nearly forty years of work and was an immediate hit. While three times more expensive than the conventional steam-powered loom, it was far more efficient, since one person could run twenty-five automatic looms simultaneously compared to two or three power looms previously. The Toyoda automatic loom was quickly adopted by the Japanese textile industry and was soon exported to both China and India.[3] Toyoda's efforts helped Japan establish itself as a textile machinery–producing nation. By 1938, the country was the main rival to Britain, the market leader. The advances made by Japan in this industry supported and enabled the development of other industries.

Toyoda accomplished his goal. He invented something that indeed encouraged the economic growth of his country. From an early age Toyoda committed his life to making a difference. Starting with nothing but the ideas in his head and his two hands, he not only helped change an industry but also a country's perception of itself. His advice to his son, Kiichiro, of what his life's work should be somehow makes the story of Sakichi Toyoda all the more remarkable. "I believe in the automobile," he told Kiichiro while he lay dying. "It will become indispensable in the future."[4] The ambition that so consumed the father was passed on to the son and with it Kiichiro built his own large life, establishing the Toyota Motor Corporation.

●   ●   ●

While the story of Sakichi Toyoda's life is complete and well known, there are other stories of people daring to live great lives that are still in the process of being told. In the middle of the crushing poverty, hunger, and hopelessness in the townships in South Africa, we found a vibrant human being who decided early in his career not to lead a little life.

In 1995, Taddy Blecher was busy rounding up an assortment of extremely attractive job offers outside of South Africa. He had already enjoyed success as a consultant at Monitor Company, an international consulting firm where he was voted Consultant of the Year for three years running.

However, two weeks before he was due to leave the country (with most of his possessions already packed into forty-one boxes and stored in his mother's house), Blecher endured a sleepless night, burdened by feelings about leaving his homeland, where over three-quarters of the households live below the poverty line and up to 70 percent of families do not have enough food to eat. As these emotions bubbled to the surface, he confronted them at last. He admits, "I didn't know the first thing about helping people, but thought maybe there's a 5 percent chance that I actually could do something."

Blecher was terrified at the prospect of making a sudden shift in his life. Nevertheless, by the morning, he had decided to remain in South Africa to help his country and its people realize their full potential.

Eight years later, Blecher and his three cofounders—Thembinkosi Mhlongo, Richard Peycke, and Mburu Gitonga—have built CIDA City Campus into a college with 1,100 current students from the most disadvantaged situations. It is succeeding against overwhelming odds, educating people who had given up hope, at a cost of less than one-tenth the amount most colleges must spend to be equally effective.

> In a single morning, a single hour, the CIDA story has rekindled my optimism…If I and my colleagues in the U.S. had any sense we would shut down Harvard and Stanford Business School, bring you to the U.S. and have you re-open them. And I suspect that in two and a half years you'd have a miracle there too.
>
> —Tom Peters, author [5]

We were introduced to Blecher by Lindsay Levin, executive director of Leaders' Quest, an international nonprofit organization that connects and develops leaders around the world. The group brings business, government, and academic leaders to countries such as China, India, and South Africa, where they come face-to-face with the challenges, opportunities, and leaders of these developing countries. Levin told us we would be inspired by Blecher's commitment, and she was right.

Talking to a local newspaper about his work in the townships he had spent most of his life avoiding, he said, "I love what I do. Every single night when I go to bed, it's like the last scene in a great movie—that happiness you feel inside, I feel that every day of my life."

In describing his decision not to emigrate, Blecher captured the spirit that drew us to him. "I could have emigrated and lived a little life in the United States, New Zealand, or Australia. I had fantastic job offers. I could have earned a lot of money and had an easy life, but it would have been a small life, one in which I wouldn't be making a real difference. What made me stay was the inkling that we were sitting on a gold mine of human potential in South Africa."

Blecher is a perfect example of someone who did not want to lead a little life, one of the enduring traits of leadership. We'll let Blecher explain in his own words the factors that led him to make this trait an overwhelming force for good, one that changed not only his life but the lives of thousands of others.

In his own words: Taddy Blecher

"LIKE MANY PEOPLE, I was going through life getting caught in little details. But then I thought, do I really want to live my life in a comfortable New York apartment, taking care of myself and just earning money, when instead I could perhaps change the future of my nation, a country where there is a desperate, aching, yearning need with thousands of kids nearby in starvation?"

Soon after Blecher resigned from his job, he went to see an agency that was working to improve education for youths in the townships. We asked him about his previous perception of the townships.

"I didn't know much about them, other than a general sense of the poverty. My family was fine. We just didn't want to get mixed up in that stuff. 'You'll be attacked,' we thought. It's just a different world."

Blecher told the agency he wanted to help in any way he could, even though he had no experience doing so. But he was passionate—a bit obsessed, perhaps—and spoke about his ability to rally people, to gather support for the agency's efforts.

The agency's leaders asked him if they could take a bit of time to think about it. He thought this meant a few weeks; instead, they walked across the room, talked for a few minutes, and came back and offered him a position as a director of the organization.

"One week later," says Blecher, "I was in the townships. I went into the poorest of the poor areas. It was an absolutely unbelievable experience.

"I saw the worst of humanity, but I also saw the best of humanity. I saw people who had courage unlike any I'd ever seen before. I saw communities that held together through thick and thin, surmounting obstacles that would have easily overwhelmed those in my 'old' world.

"While working with high school kids, I was often the only white guy walking around the township. Little children would grab a hold of me, wanting to touch my head because of my 'different' hair. The kids were very innocent, and it touched my heart in an incredible manner. The children brought me poetry they'd written and recited it. Their words and their eyes were full of hope for a better future."

Working in the townships gave Blecher a fresh perspective. For the first time, he saw that many people, whether deliberately or not, shield themselves from the problems that persist around them. "We have these big houses, these big walls. We have electrified fences. We get into our cars, lock the doors, and drive straight to work. We park our cars in a safe, secure basement with security. At the end of the day, we drive straight back home.

"Suddenly I was in a completely different world. I went to funerals and I went to weddings. I cried and laughed and gained a fuller sense of what life is like for millions of people in this country.

"Initially and on the surface, some people appear to be people you wouldn't want to know . . . someone who doesn't want to become anything. But if you look close enough and take the time to become familiar with what they are really made of, you can see in them the potential to become something precious. And then, with more patience, you can help them move away from the notion that they cannot become anything else . . . you can help them believe in themselves, their worth, their future.

"The first thing, though, is that you must believe that the potential is there. We see this lack of belief in many of our modern organizations. We say we trust our people, but then we keep checking on them every two minutes. We say we want a person to be responsible, but we don't really give them responsibility. And so I think believing in people is the critical starting point."

With this sort of attitude, Blecher and his colleagues educated disadvantaged township children—helping to raise their grades, stop alcohol and drug abuse, and escape physical violence—and taught them to help each other.

After some years of incremental change and growing success, high school graduates started coming back to Blecher, claiming they could not find a job and had no means to get into college. They were stuck in a trap, and that trap threatened to undo all the positive things his team was achieving.

True to form, rather than becoming discouraged Blecher and his colleagues got the "crazy idea" to start a college that would educate these kids at one-tenth or less of the cost of other colleges. The college was created to teach them how to start businesses and ignite an economic engine that would help break the cycle of poverty, as well as instill in each student a responsibility to educate and help their community.

Again, they had no money and no experience. But they had one huge advantage: the determination not to settle for a little, protected life.

The story of the founding and flourishing of CIDA City Campus could fill an entire book. In 2004, CIDA has 1,100 students, each on a tuition scholarship. Over the next five years, they hope to have 5,000 to 9,000 students in their Johannesburg city center campus, and then to replicate CIDA in other provinces. The college is funded mainly by the South African private sector. Professors from MIT, Harvard, Berkeley, the London School of Economics and others have visited to better understand CIDA's innovative approach.

Blecher explains what it takes to lead such a change. "You must build and build and build, and the beginning is the hardest part. And you've got to believe night and day, and nothing can stop you. Obstacles will present themselves daily, and some will say you are crazy, while others will be negative. Without belief, you'll give up. You have to take all the blows and keep going. If you do, you will begin to succeed. Those successes will sustain you further. But you must never give up."

•   •   •

Two critical elements are present in Blecher's comments, both of which are universal to those who do not want to live a small life. The first is the decision to make a difference. The second, which is more important, is the determination to succeed no matter what.

Whether you call this determination, tenacity, relentlessness, or something else, it is what separates leaders from dreamers. Many of us dream of changing the world or at least our corner of it, but far fewer actually make it happen. The difference is whether you are able to view every obstacle as surmountable.

The determination to make a difference and to succeed in doing so is a rare quality. But is it innate or learned? Are people born with such drive or do they acquire it over a lifetime of experiences? And if the latter, do a person's drive and commitment evolve from one major transforming experience or are they due to a series of events?

The decision to make a difference has come later in life for more leaders than we imagined. Take for example Dave Pottruck, CEO of Charles Schwab & Co., Inc., who admits he was in graduate school before recognizing that he was aiming too low.

"I wanted to be a pro athlete," Pottruck told us, "but it was not a goal; it was a dream. Goals are dreams with deadlines. I had the dream but no way of getting there and no real belief that I could.

"I received a letter from the Miami Dolphins offering me the opportunity to try out for a position on the team. I had been the most valuable player on my college football team. I was one step away from All-American in wrestling, in the top ten in the country. But I didn't think I was good enough to be a pro football player, so I didn't show up for the tryouts. I went to graduate school instead.

"I had played football against a guy, Doug Swift, who, like me, didn't go to a big football school. He went to Amherst. And, like me, he was the best player on his team. He also received a similar letter from the Dolphins. Unlike me, Doug showed up and went on to start as linebacker, the same position I played. He was the starting linebacker for the Miami Dolphins for ten years and played in two Super Bowls.[6]

"Every time I saw Doug on television, I thought to myself, 'Well, that might have been me. That might have been me.' But I had given myself zero chance by not showing up. It stared me in the face, this guy who went on to achieve what I did not.

"I decided that I wasn't going to do that anymore. I wasn't going to limit my goals by believing that I wasn't able to achieve them. I became determined to give it my best. I decided to set very high goals for myself and realized that if I didn't make it, there's no great shame in that. In fact, I would be a better person for having tried."

We see these pivotal moments again and again in the lives of successful leaders. Sometimes these moments provide meaning in a person's life, as for Toyoda; other times they bring about a change in direction, as for Taddy Blecher; while other times they spark greater determination, as they did for Dave Pottruck.

Our point is that you have the ability to make such a decision in your own life. "To change others, change yourself," says University of Pennsylvania's Wharton School of Business faculty member Kenwyn Smith.[7] We have far greater capacity for change than most of us recognize, and often the only lacking element is our own willingness to initiate the change we desire.

Mary Kay Ash, founder of Mary Kay Inc, which had sales of $1.6 billion in 2002, spent eleven years working as director of sales training for a firm, only to be devastated when a male subordinate was promoted to be her boss at twice her salary. Ash started working on a book about what she had gone through. Then, she said, "I began asking myself, 'Why are you theorizing about a dream company? Why don't you just start one?'" After buying a formulation for a skin-care cream, Ash enlisted her husband to handle operations and began recruiting friends to be beauty consultants for the venture she called "Beauty by Mary Kay."[8]

She invested all her savings into the venture, only to have her husband die suddenly a month before the company's doors were set to open. She went ahead anyway at age forty-five.

So the woman whom John Kotter, a leading expert on leadership, has called one of the best business leaders in the United States, didn't commit to change her life until she was halfway through her fifth decade.[9]

Leadership comes in many forms. When disasters strike, some people inevitably rise to the challenge and give far more of themselves than anyone thought possible. The examples of this type of leadership serve as powerful reminders of what we are capable of achieving. More often than not, character is revealed in times of crisis.

> We didn't know if it was humanly possible to reach the top of Mt. Everest. And even using oxygen as we were, if we did get to the top, we weren't at all sure whether we wouldn't drop dead or something of that nature. . . .
>
> I have very modest abilities. Academically I was very modest. Mediocre perhaps, and I think perhaps physically I did not have a great athletic sense, but I was big and strong. I think the only thing in which I was less than modest was in motivation. I really wanted very strongly to do many of these things and once I started I didn't give up all that easily.
>
> —Sir Edmund Hillary, conqueror of Mt. Everest[10]

Rudolph Giuliani, former mayor of New York City, is widely perceived to have done an extraordinary job providing leadership after 9/11, not only for New York City but also for millions of others affected by the terrorist attacks. In both his careers, as a federal prosecutor and as mayor of New York City, Giuliani made a commitment to leading a life that made a difference, but this may not have been widely appreciated until the days and weeks that followed the 9/11 tragedy.

As *Time* magazine said in naming him 2001's Person of the Year, "The first Republican to run the town in a generation, he had restored New York's spirit, cutting crime by two-thirds, moving 691,000 people off the welfare rolls, boosting property values and incomes in neighborhoods rich and poor, redeveloping great swaths of the city. But great swaths of the city were sick of him. People were sick of his Vesuvian temper and constant battles."[11]

Many people forget that September 11, 2001, was supposed to be the day when Giuliani became a lame duck; it was primary election day for the mayor's race, and due to term limits, Giuliani was not running. Instead, September 11 became the day his leadership skills emerged more vital and welcomed than ever.

What causes people to shine in such situations? One explanation is that that they previously decided to live a certain kind of life, one in which they will step forward when others are in need or when tough situations arise that others cannot handle. Because they have already made a commitment, it is actually easier for them to risk their own safety and contribute extraordinary efforts than to turn their backs on situations that call for their leadership and dedication.

When the business writer Jim Collins named the ten greatest CEOs of all time in an article he wrote for *Fortune* magazine, he placed former Johnson & Johnson CEO James Burke at number six, but not for the reason most of us would think. To Collins, what made Burke an outstanding leader was not his decision to remove Tylenol capsules from the shelves in reaction to the cyanide-poisoning crisis of 1982. It was something that had occurred three years earlier.

Taking twenty senior executives into a conference room, Burke asked whether the then thirty-six year-old Johnson & Johnson credo had become an artifact—if, in fact, it was still relevant for the company to take on that part of the document that said the company had a higher duty to "mothers and all others who use [its] product."[12] Stunned into silence, the executives were not sure if Burke was joking. After realizing that the CEO was quite serious, they decided that the document should be seen as essential to how the company's business would be conducted in the future, all over the world.

Collins writes that while no one could have predicted the tragedies of 1982, the manner in which Burke and Johnson & Johnson would react to such events was predictable. There would be no discussions about whether customer safety outweighed financial considerations. That people mattered most was a given; Burke and Johnson & Johnson would do what was right.[13]

Again and again we have come across leaders who can identify the point in their lives when they made conscious decisions to dedicate themselves to making a difference, or when they realized how much more worthwhile their lives could be than they had originally believed.

Colin Powell, former chairman of the Joint Chiefs of Staff and currently United States secretary of state, was born in Harlem and started out as an average student. In his autobiography, Powell admits he was "directionless" in high school. But he made it to the City College of New York, and after joining ROTC he pledged the most elite of the three military societies on campus, the Pershing Rifles.

Powell writes, "The discipline, the structure, the camaraderie, the sense of belonging were what I craved. I became a leader almost immediately. I found a selflessness within our ranks that reminded me of the caring atmosphere within my family. Race, color, background, income meant nothing. The PRs would go the limit for each other and for the group."[14]

For Powell, finding a second family cultivated his leadership abilities. He committed to be a valuable member of the "family," one on whom others could depend.

In his highly engaging biography of John Adams, David McCullough relates that Adams, too, spent time drifting. After completing Harvard in 1755, he went to Worcester, Massachusetts, on the first step toward becoming a lawyer. During this time, Adams kept a journal, which provides a window into his own self-doubts.

McCullough summarizes some of Adams' musings: "Why was he so constantly forming yet never executing good resolutions? Why was he so absent-minded, so lazy, so prone to daydreaming his life away? He vowed to read more seriously. He vowed to quit chewing tobacco." But Adams quickly broke or forgot many of these resolutions.

Only after becoming a lawyer and then feeling humiliated when he lost his first case on a technicality did Adams vow, as McCullough writes, to "bend his whole soul to the law." His diary was soon filled with observations he made regarding practices of the best attorneys, and Adams became the busiest attorney in Boston while still in his thirties.[15]

In their younger years, Powell, Adams, and most of us certainly missed opportunities to be leaders, or to get the most out of our lives. There is no way to rectify the situation now.

What we can do, however, is learn that true leadership often revolves around a decision—a commitment—that can be made at any point in life. If you have made such a commitment, you are well on your way. If you have not yet done so, there is nothing stopping you but yourself.

• • •

"It isn't like I knew exactly what I wanted to do, but one thing I did know was that I wanted to make a difference." So says Klaus Kleinfeld, member of the Corporate Executive Committee at Siemens AG, and formerly president and CEO of Siemens Corporation of New York, when thinking of his boyhood aspirations.

Recalling one of his favorite jobs growing up, Kleinfeld continues,

> The program was one that entertained children whose families' did not have enough money to go on summer vacation. We would often inherit the facilities of schools or other social venues. In that first summer, we were in a very poor neighborhood. The facility was literally the home of a motorcycle gang, the members of which were always getting drunk and beating each other up. We, of course, had to figure out a way of handling them.
>
> My team was about six, seven people and I was one of the youngest. But interestingly, as we tried to figure out what we were going to do with the gang, it became clear to me that everyone was looking to me for advice and suggestions. So I said that I didn't think we should chase the motorcycle gang away, that it would be better if we integrated them into what we were trying to do. I thought, perhaps, that we could leave a mark on them.
>
> So we literally became friends with them. It was a super summer. It was great to integrate them into the program. They did great things with our kids. They enjoyed it. They never admitted it. And then when we left at around six in the evening, they still got drunk, but you can only change so much. But I think we left an impression on them.

• • •

Perhaps more important for readers of this book—many of whom we expect have already demonstrated their leadership skills—you are in a position to inspire others to use their lives well. Thinking again of Sakichi Toyoda's dying words to his son, and knowing what resulted, you can better understand that by expressing confidence in your children, employees, and colleagues, you have the potential to inspire them to aim higher, work harder, and persevere longer. If you can help them reach the point where they make a true commitment not to lead a little life, then most other things will fall into place.

It may be a cliché, but if you can find a spark inside another human being, it is well worth your time to tend the flame and help it burn brighter.

sources

1. *The Forbes Book of Business Quotations*, ed. Ted Goodman (New York: Black Dog & Leventhal Publishers, 1997), p. 399.2.

2. Selected quote, "Ambition," http://www.quotationreference.com/quotefinder.php?strt =1&subj =Thomas+Stearns+Eliot&byax=1&lr=A (accessed February 12, 2004).

3. Jeffrey R. Bernstein, "Toyoda Automatic Looms and Toyota Automobiles," in *Creating Modern Capitalism: How Entrepreneurs Companies, and Countries Triumphed in Three Industrial Revolutions*, ed. Thomas K. McCraw, (Cambridge, MA: Harvard University Press, 1997), p. 403.

4. Ibid., p. 407.

5. Ethel Hazelhurst, "Seeing Is Believing the New Education Miracle" (includes comments by Tom Peters), *Financial Mail*, November 8, 2002.

6. A fine arts major at Amherst, while playing for the Miami Dolphins, Doug Swift completed premed course work. After retiring from football, he attended medical school at the University of Pennsylvania and is presently a practicing anesthesiologist. He, too, has committed himself to leading a very interesting life.

7. Premise used to describe course taught within leadership program at University of Pennsylvania's Wharton School of Business, http://leadership.wharton.upenn.edu/digest/10-98.shtml (accessed February 22, 2004).

8. Mary Kay, Inc.'s official website, "Biography Mary Kay Ash," http://www.marykay.com/ Headquarters/MaryKayBiography/Biography2.asp (accessed February 22, 2004).

9. Alan Farnham, "Mary Kay's Lessons in Leadership," *Fortune*, September 20, 1993.

10. Selected quote, "Ambition," http://www.achievement.org/autodoc/steps/per?index=34 (accessed February 15, 2004).

11. Eric Pooley, "Mayor of the World, *Time*, December 31, 2001–January 7, 2002, p. 40.

12. Jim Collins, "The 10 Greatest CEOs of All Time," *Fortune*, July 21, 2003, p. 62.

13. Ibid.

14. Colin Powell, *My American Journey*, with Joseph E. Persico (New York: Random House, 1995).

15. David McCullough, *John Adams* (New York: Simon & Schuster, 2001).

2

Vision

Vision without action is a daydream.
Action without vision is a nightmare.
—Japanese proverb[1]

To build a motor car for the great multitude . . . It will be so low in price that no man making a good salary will be unable to own one—and enjoy with his family the blessing of hours of pleasure in God's great open spaces . . . everybody will be able to afford one, and everyone will have one. The horse will have disappeared from our highways, the automobile will be taken for granted.
—Henry Ford[2]

TO LEAD OTHERS, you must have a destination in mind and then you must have a plan to get there. This is what we mean by vision.

More important, you must be absolutely committed to making the vision that you embrace come true. When people in leadership positions fail, it is often because they bounce from one vision to another, making it impossible for others to follow or for any of their goals to come to fruition.

Your vision will be buffeted from all sides, tested, and threatened. This is why you must be fully committed to it and ready not only to defend it, but also to convince others to nurture it as their own.

So much of the business literature over the past twenty years has been devoted to strategy or strategy development. While sound strategy is critical to the success of any good business, it is not something that always originates in the mind of a leader. Strategy can be, and has often been, taken from other sources.

In ancient Rome, the great victories of Octavian over the far more experienced Marc Antony were not a result of the former's tactical skills, but instead were a consequence of Octavian placing his trust in the strategic abilities of his general, Agrippa. Today, the success of many companies is the result of hiring and implementing the recommendations of consulting firms such as McKinsey & Company and The Boston Consulting Group. Simply being able to strategize does not necessarily make a good leader. Octavian, as Caesar Augustus, is recognized as one of history's greatest leaders, but he was a great politician with a vision, not a great strategist. What was more important to him, and what could not be taken from someone else, was vision. For Octavian, that vision was to be the emperor of Rome.

Vision transcends strategy—it is a sixth sense, the awareness of what will exist prior to it actually existing, the ability to "see around the corners." Having a vision does not always mean being a visionary. While we may be splitting hairs, we believe this is fundamental to understanding great leadership. Great leaders may adopt their vision from visionaries, and they may have strategists develop the path to achieving the vision. However, great leaders cannot delegate two things: believing in the vision and inspiring others to share that vision. In addition, great leaders have the instincts to know a good vision when they see one and the good sense to surround themselves with people who may know more about achieving the vision than they do.

We believe that most great leaders share three traits: drive and commitment (addressed in the previous chapter), vision, and the ability to communicate (see the next chapter). Joining this trifecta to enhance and distinguish leadership capabilities are the additional traits treated in Chapters 4 through 9. In this chapter, we want to clarify why vision is so important, how it manifests itself, and how we recognize vision.

Robert Johnson is the founder, chairman, and CEO of Black Entertainment Television (BET), now a subsidiary of Viacom. He has long been recognized as the man who was able not only to successfully introduce but also to sustain an urban voice on American television. As a result, he has played a seminal role in the acceptance of African-American sensibilities into the mainstream. He is the first to admit that his success was in part due to luck and being in the right place at the right time. But he also thinks it the result of other things, particularly a vision for what he wanted to do with his life.

In his own words: Robert Johnson

"WHEN YOU ASK about vision, I think it began for me in childhood with the desire to work for myself. I always liked the idea of being my own boss. Or to put it another way, I didn't like anybody else being my boss. So if you're not going to let somebody else boss you, then you better come up with your own way of making money.

"First, there was the interest of wanting to get an understanding of how African-Americans were depicted in images. I was aware of a number of organizations at the time that were making arguments about how best to provide content directed to minorities so that they would get their share of voice. And, of course, there were already models out there that were providing diversity of voices and diversity of content for African-Americans. In the print business, it was John Johnson and *Ebony*. Black radio had done it for a long time. But no one had put it together with television. So BET was derived from the idea of wanting to create a television channel that catered to the interests of the African-American community."

But how to make money on such a venture was not immediately clear to Johnson. Not until the late 1970s, when cable began to change the media landscape, did he began to think that BET could actually exist.

"I was working as a lobbyist for the cable television industry. Cable was still in its infancy. So it was sort of right time, right place in terms of a technology getting ready to grow beyond being a fundamental sort of a retransmission product to a communications product.

"In addition, cable operators were beginning to move into urban markets. However, before those communities awarded them franchises, the African-American city council members were intent on making sure that the kind of programming offered would be in line with the sensibilities of the community. In an environment like this, what I wanted to do became more realistic and possible."

Thus, unexpected circumstances, the right timing, or a bit of luck are often necessary for a vision to be realized. However, for a vision to succeed, leaders must possess the skills necessary to gain from these rare, serendipitous moments, or have the good sense to surround themselves with people who do. Having a clear vision of what one is trying to accomplish is often an essential tool to finding necessary support.

Aside from Johnson himself, the person most responsible for the early growth of BET was John Malone. Johnson talks below about how he was able to secure the cable executive's assistance:

"Malone was with the third-largest cable operator at that time. He was recognized as one of the smartest guys in the industry. And when he invested in BET, he fundamentally gave me a good housekeeping seal, which really made my life easier. Malone opened a lot of doors for me, and that was critical.

"[Malone's] support was the result of two things. First of all, he had an affinity for entrepreneurs: the ones whose vision he believed in. Second, and this was probably the more important of the two, he had cable systems in urban markets, and he wanted to get programming that would help him get more subscribers to sign up.

"So when I went to him with the idea, he asked how much I would need. I said I needed half a million dollars. He said, 'I'll tell you what I'll do Bob,— and this took place in about a thirty-five minute conversation—I'll buy 20 percent of your company for $180 [thousand] and I'll loan you $320 [thousand]. And you'll be 80 percent and I'll be 20 percent. Is that a deal?'

"Of course it was. Later on I asked him why he structured a deal that gave him only 20 percent of the company after he put in all of the money. And he said, 'Bob, I knew that you would work harder for yourself than you would for me.'"

Aside from the role in building and finding support for BET, Johnson's vision played a large part in his decision to take the company public. It was always a goal of his for BET to be the first African-American company listed on the New York Stock Exchange. Johnson explains:

"I have always liked the idea of being first in a category. If you're first in a category, particularly if you're a minority, you get spillover benefits. That is, recognition comes your way that propels you to other opportunities. So it was always a part of my vision, one that I may not have always expressed, to be the first to do something in this category."

Vision is a tool used either to further advancement or to stave off weakness. Vision usually begins with one or a small number of people. Its realization requires the assistance of a far greater number—the majority of whom have to move from what is comfortable and known to something that is altogether different.

Perhaps one of the most famous contemporary examples of vision was first articulated in New York City, at the Hotel Pierre, on December 8, 1981. Jack Welch was giving his first presentation to the financial community as the CEO of General Electric (GE), and his message was, to say the least, different. Instead of talking about GE's performance over the past year, Welch spoke about the companies that would succeed and fail in the coming years. The winners would "search out and participate in the real growth industries and insist on being number one or number two in every business they are in—the number one or two leanest, lowest-cost, worldwide producers of quality goods and services. . . . The managements and companies of the eighties that don't do this, that hang on to losers for whatever reason—tradition, sentiment, their own management weaknesses—won't be around in 1990." [3]

Welch was a student of business management guru and author Peter Drucker. And at the time of his presentation, inflation was threatening to drastically reduce economic growth worldwide. Welch took what he had learned from Drucker and applied it to the situation that GE was facing. In so doing, he created his vision for the company. The lack of future growth opportunities resulting from inflation necessitated that GE, if it was going to stay healthy, be either number one or two in all of the industries in which it participated. Welch's vision was for GE to be a leader in all of the industries in which GE was involved.

This was a lofty goal, and though GE was in robust health at the time, the prevailing realities did not guarantee that would remain the case. GE could have faltered as a result of inflation. But due in part to Welch's vision, the company shifted its priorities and became stronger.

Like Welch did at GE, Wm. Wrigley Jr. Company chairman and CEO William Wrigley Jr. has turned vision into the tool by which his company can advance its interests while compensating for "potential" shortcomings. In speaking to us, Wrigley noted that he tended to be someone who spent time focusing on the future of the company, and developing a long-term view. He noted that, like Welch, his creation of a vision was not a reaction to any immediate threats to the company, but more the result of his interest in seeing what the Wm. Wrigley Jr. Company could become.

Wrigley told us, "We've had a lot of change here over the last four years. And to do that, we didn't use the burning-platform approach. The reasons were, one, I don't believe in emphasizing the negative, and two, we didn't have a burning platform here. While there had had been a drop-off in business around the time I arrived, which was 1999, there had also been numerous successes. Our challenge was more in envisioning how we could change so that the company could benefit and continue to grow."

Wrigley's solution, though plain in appearance, has had a dramatic impact on how the company, in recent years, has defined its strategy and approached the markets. "In words, this vision is pretty simple: Wrigley brands woven into the fabric of everyday life around the world. But it's much more than words or a rallying cry. We use it as a filter to guide our decision making. When we're making an important strategic decision or wondering whether to partner on something, we ask ourselves first if, by taking this action, we are furthering the case for Wrigley brands. Are we doing something with these new distribution channels to really weave the Wrigley name into the fabric of everyday life?

"As time goes on, the end result of this will be a company that is more than a chewing gum company. And for a company that's been characterized by chewing gum for much of the last hundred years, it is a big shift to go into the much broader confectionary category."

●　　●　　●

While having a vision is important for a leader, the word itself has become a bit of a catchphrase, becoming much abused, especially in light of Welch's success at GE. The most famous statement in recent years against vision came from Louis Gerstner shortly after he took over leadership of IBM. It caused quite a bit of controversy.

Gerstner recently recalled, "When I said in August of 1993 that the last thing IBM needed was a vision, I was thrown into the stocks, pilloried and beaten and sort of described as an incompetent."[4]

In truth, Gerstner faced daunting, immediate challenges. Reuters reports:

> Gerstner became chairman and chief executive of IBM in April 1993. In 1992 and 1993, the company had a combined net loss of about $13 billion, which put Big Blue in a position to flirt with bankruptcy.[5]

Gerstner did have a vision, but what he discouraged was his subordinates getting diverted by a bureaucratic and tedious "visioning" process. Many companies have devoted millions of dollars and hundreds of hours to the construction of the perfect vision, mission and strategy statements and not enough to taking the difficult actions necessary to drive needed change. Gerstner knew he had to change the culture at IBM for the company to rapidly improve its ability to execute effectively.

Whether you are the CEO of IBM or GE or the founder of a company no one outside of your immediate family has ever heard of, utter commitment to a vision can overcome nearly any obstacle. Just ask Rupert Murdoch, the chairman and CEO of News Corporation.

Murdoch had long wanted control over the distribution of the content—film, news, and television—created by News Corp. The outcome of this vision was an ever-expanding satellite network, where the company oversaw the delivery of its content in most major world markets. One market, however, remained elusive, and it offered the greatest opportunity.

Cable companies controlled the distribution of paid television content in the United States, frustrating Murdoch to no end during the launch of Fox News in America. And while now very successful, during Fox News's infancy, Murdoch had to bully, coax, and beg the cable operators in order to gain access to their lines.

To counter the cable companies' leverage, Murdoch spent much of the 1980s and 1990s trying to bypass them altogether. (Acquisition did not make sense since the underlying technology was not one Murdoch was fully committed to; he thought there were better alternatives.) Therefore, as he did elsewhere, Murdoch focused on finding a U.S.-based satellite TV distribution platform.

Two satellite distributors existed in the United States—EchoStar and DirecTV, owned by Hughes Electronics, which was a subsidiary of General Motors (GM). Murdoch focused on DirecTV. It was larger, and he felt GM was a more pliant negotiator than EchoStar's management team, which was led by the company's founder, Charles Ergen.

At first, GM proved a hesitant partner, but in September 2000 talks between the two companies intensified. By August 2001, the GM board was ready to vote on Murdoch's offer, which had valued Hughes Electronics (DirecTV's immediate parent) at $22.5 billion.[6]

With the purchase of DirecTV, Murdoch would finally be able to circumvent the obstacles posed by the U.S. cable companies. His dream, however, was again put on hold. On August 5, 2001, Ergen trumped Murdoch and made an unsolicited bid for Hughes that GM eventually accepted.

Further frustrating Murdoch's attempts to realize his vision, in February 2002, News Corp. was forced to write off its investment in Germany's KirchMedia Group, a leading player in the European pay television market. In addition, the company was forced to reduce the value of its 42 percent stake in Gemstar, the U.S. interactive television guide, by $6.9 billion as result of Gemstar's involvement in a series of accounting scandals. All told, in 2001, News Corp. posted the largest loss in Australian corporate history, $12 billion.[7]

By all outward appearances, Rupert Murdoch's long-held vision for his company would go unrealized. However, despite the problems he faced, Murdoch would not allow himself to feel defeated. Too much of an optimist, he became a tireless visitor to Washington, D.C., lobbying to have the FCC block the EchoStar-Hughes deal, which the FCC did in October 2002.

Murdoch reacted quickly and decisively—he was not going to let DirectTV (and his vision) be taken away from him again. On April 9, 2003, News Corp. announced that it paid $6.6 billion for a 34 percent stake in Hughes Electronics.[8] The price was drastically lower than what both Murdoch and Ergen had offered almost two years before, perhaps a fitting reward for Murdoch's patience and commitment.

We hope you see a clear difference between the type of vision we see in effective leaders versus any business-speak efforts to craft vision statements. Statements can be merely two-dimensional shadows of the leadership trait we describe in this chapter, simple words on paper. To bring them to life, a leader must vest his or her whole being in leading others down the path ahead. You may question whether Murdoch's victory was a good thing; you cannot question how important vision was to his success.

On May 25, 1961, President John F. Kennedy went before a joint session of Congress to present his vision that the country could put a man on the moon before the end of that decade. "I believe that this nation should commit itself to achieving the goal," proclaimed Kennedy, "before this decade is out, of landing a man on the moon and returning him safely to the earth."

Locked in an arms race with the Soviet Union, grappling with the aftermath of the Bay of Pigs fiasco, the president stated, "No single space project in this period will be more impressive to mankind, or more important for the long-range exploration of space; and none will be so difficult or expensive to accomplish."[9]

Many people thought this goal was absurd, but on July 20, 1969, Neil Armstrong took his famous first step, making Kennedy's vision come true.

Not long after Kennedy began America's race for the moon, Nelson Mandela was imprisoned in South Africa, where he remained for twenty-seven years. Even during his imprisonment, he was committed to a vision with intensity perhaps unmatched by anyone else. In a speech in 1963, he said, "I have fought against white domination, and I have fought against black domination. I have cherished the ideal of a democratic and free society in which all persons live together in harmony and with equal opportunities."[11]

> Don't underestimate the power of a vision. McDonald's founder, Ray Kroc, pictured his empire long before it existed, and he saw how to get there. He invented the company motto—"Quality, service, cleanliness, and value"—and kept repeating it to employees for the rest of his life.
>
> —*Fortune*, 1989[10]

More than thirty years later, after spending nearly three decades in prison, he negotiated the end of the apartheid regime and became South Africa's first black president in 1994. Then he began building a government that remained faithful to this vision. Few others would have had the capacity to avoid bitterness.

In 1993, when accepting the Nobel Peace Prize, Mandela spoke of his vision:

> At the southern tip of the continent of Africa, a rich reward is in the making, an invaluable gift is in the preparation for those who suffered in the name of all humanity when they sacrificed everything for liberty, peace, human dignity and human fulfillment.
>
> This reward will not be measured in money. Nor can it be reckoned in the collective price of the rare metals and precious stones that rest in the bowels of the African soil we tread in the footsteps of our ancestors.

It will and must be measured by the happiness and welfare of the children, at once the most vulnerable citizens in any society and the greatest of our treasures.

The children must, at last, play in the open field, no longer tortured by the pangs of hunger or ravaged by disease or threatened with the scourge of ignorance, molestation and abuse, and no longer required to engage in deeds whose gravity exceeds the demands of their tender years.[12]

We share this story with you for two reasons. First, because Mandela is a wonderful example of a man who remained true to his vision and convinced others to embrace that vision. Second, because his story demonstrates that making a vision come true can take much longer than you hope, and that the presence of overwhelming obstacles is no reason to abandon a vision in which you deeply believe.

• • •

On June 5, 1947, U.S. secretary of state George Marshall gave the commencement address at Harvard University. Reporters present that day were told that the speech would be nothing but routine and they treated it as such. But if they had listened , they would have realized that Marshall's words were far from routine. It was a vision of how Europe would recover from the horrors that were inflicted upon it during the Second World War. What follows are selected excerpts of what Marshall said that day, the first mention of what Winston Churchill would later call the "most unsordid political act in history."[13]

> In considering the requirements for the rehabilitation of Europe, the physical loss of life, the visible destruction of cities, factories, mines, and railroads was correctly estimated, but it has become obvious during recent months that this visible destruction was probably less serious than the dislocation of the entire fabric of European economy. . . .The feverish preparation for war and the more feverish maintenance of the war effort engulfed all aspects of national economies. . . . Long-standing commercial ties, private institutions, banks, insurance companies, and shipping companies disappeared through loss of capital, absorption through nationalization, or by simple destruction. . .
>
> The truth of the matter is that Europe's requirements for the next

three or four years of foreign food and other essential products—principally from America—are so much greater than her present ability to pay that she must have substantial additional help or face economic, social, and political deterioration of a very grave character.

The remedy lies in breaking the vicious circle and restoring the confidence of the European people in the economic future of their own countries and of Europe as a whole...

It is logical that the United States should do whatever it is able to do to assist in the return of normal economic health in the world, without which there can be no political stability and no assured peace. Our policy is directed not against any country or doctrine but against hunger, poverty, desperation, and chaos. Its purpose should be the revival of a working economy in the world so as to permit the emergence of political and social conditions in which free institutions can exist. Such assistance, I am convinced, must not be on a piecemeal basis as various crises develop. Any assistance that this Government may render in the future should provide a cure rather than a mere palliative. [14]

What was Marshall's intent that day when he offered these words? Was it to rally people to a cause to which he was committed? Certainly. But what was the cause? The recovery of Europe for sure, but it can be argued that that was just a means to an end. Marshall's words were spoken in response to the growing voice of communism heard in most postwar European countries. Marshall wanted to stop the spread of communism. And while this is the simple answer to a complex question, it is nevertheless true. Marshall was all too familiar with what had happened after World War I when countries were forced to pay heavy reparations for their roles in the conflict. They suffered horribly and became marginalized, allowing for splinter groups like the Nazis to grow in power and influence. Marshall knew that by assisting in the recovery of Europe, the United States would, in all likelihood, be preventing history from repeating itself; communism would have far more difficulty finding an audience in a prosperous and healthy Europe than it would in a broken one.

There was genius in Marshall's address at Harvard. And it is one that exists in many strong visions. That is, responding to something that has not yet presented itself—seeing what exists around the bend. Marshall was reacting to what he saw as the advance of communism and he offered a way to stop it. This foresight is essential if a vision is to be realized. If it does not exist, then often people are left unequipped to deal with the unknown.

George Marshall's vision was introduced in 1947, and while it is most likely known what followed from his address, some things are still worth mentioning. From around the world there was immediate support of his proposal. Representatives of many European nations, including, interestingly enough, the Soviet Union, met in Paris to talk about "the Marshall Plan." While the communist delegates quickly removed themselves from the proceedings, most of Western Europe plus Turkey and Greece remained enthusiastic about the American offer of aid. Soon the Organization for European Economic Cooperation (OEEC) was formed. The OEEC's mission was to increase production, control inflation, and promote European economic cooperation by lowering trade barriers. To assure the success of these goals, and the European countries' movement toward a better life, the United States sent $13 billion in food, machinery, and other products to its allies.[15]

The Marshall Plan came to its end in 1951, the initial vision having been realized. The economies of the seventeen countries whose membership formed the OEEC were on the road to recovery. In addition, the plan has been recognized as having a severe impact on the then emerging communist parties of Western Europe.

●   ●   ●

To understand how a team of leaders were able to stay true to a vision over twenty years of growth, we spoke with Nandan Nilekani, CEO and managing director of Infosys Technologies, Ltd., a global software firm based in India. Today, its clients are the biggest and best firms in the world, but for much of its life the firm was a small company with a big vision. If you pay close attention to the first words Nilekani shares in the section below, he describes that vision immediately: to be a global firm respected and known the world over.

The firm has stayed true to the cofounders' vision through years when it probably seemed absurd to think that this small firm in India could compete on the world stage. Infosys grew 13-fold from 1994 to 1999, as revenues increased from $9.5 million to $125.6 million. In the fiscal year closing March 2003, the firm's revenues were $753 million, and it is projected that the company will surpass $1 billion in 2004.[16]

In his own words: Nandan Nilekani

"INFOSYS WAS FOUNDED in 1981 by a group of seven software professionals with the intent and ambition to create a global software company that was respected and known the world over. We had about two to three hundred dollars among the seven of us, but it was set up to be a professional company, with a strong value system.

"From day one we were all working for the same cause. It's important for the success of a company to have a clear vision of what you want the company to be. All of us—the founders of Infosys—are willing to subsume our egos and our individual aspirations for a larger goal. It's certainly the key to building the future. Having people who believe in building a future together is more important than personal goals. But also, we each need to feel the excitement.

"We wanted our company to be very employee-oriented and a place where people would come to work and prosper. The idealism of moving the Indian talent pool into a global economy and creating a wealth of IT services was the foundation of our company.

"It's been twenty-two years since we set up the company and this year our revenues will be over a billion dollars. We have more than 22,000 employees. In India, we are recognized as the most admired company and the best employer. We have set the bar in getting global interest in India and in Indian [outsourcing].

"We were at the right place with the right value proposition at the right time. More and more countries are trying to develop market economies and become part of the global economy. Technology has simply made it possible to completely reconfigure how we deliver service to customers."

For Infosys a vision has come to fruition after twenty years of hard work, but during that time, the firm encountered numerous obstacles, certainly more than enough to shake many leaders' resolve.

Nilekani admits, "We had very tough times. We were a small company and we were unknown. We didn't have capital. It was tough to convince customers about what we could do. Technology then wasn't what it is today, and India had many restrictions on how to invest the money.

"But we had this burning desire to create a different kind of firm. When you are talking about leadership, it's an asset to see a future that is quite different from and better than today. Then you can start believing that you can achieve in your life the things you have connected to that future. Doing so gives you emotional fuel and energy and resilience to deal with short-term obstacles or short-term setbacks."

From day one, the company's founders shared a vision of creating a firm that could attract the best employees, by offering them a brighter future than they could expect elsewhere. The founders recognized that their growth was dependent on their own people, and that the company's value system had to be unique. To that end, the firm has cultivated a brand that is increasingly synonymous in India with these goals.

We asked Nilekani what excites him.

"What drives me," he responded, "is that I can see the future in the sense that I know that we can do much, much better in the way we serve our customers. The future can be much better for our employees. And I do whatever I can to make that future happen. Also, I think that trying to make a difference and make it better will make my own life more meaningful."

A strong vision can lead firms to take extraordinary steps to stay on course, steps that might seem untenable to other competitors. In 2000, the company was growing at a rate of 68 percent; in 2001, growth was 103.4 percent; in 2002, growth dropped to 30 percent.

Nilekani explains, "We invest in the people in the sense that the employee is the most valuable asset. We overhired, but then the bubble burst and we found that we had a lot of people on our hands who didn't have any work . . . and we felt responsible to keep them on the payroll. These are very bright young people who have joined us in the hope that things would go well, and we recognized that we could afford to keep paying them, and so we kept them on board."

This dedication to employees as well as to customers paid off. In 2002, Hewitt Associates, an international management consulting firm, named Infosys India's Best Employer, and in 2003 DC-IDC recognized the firm as being the "dream company for IT employees in India." [17]

None of this means that Infosys is ignoring the bottom line. To cope with the slowdown in growth, Nilekani also focused on productivity improvements, cost reductions, and delivering more value to customers for their IT investments. [18]

We asked Nilekani how the leaders of a firm communicate a vision to 22,000 employees.

"It's a constant challenge. The challenge of leadership is learning how you can motivate, energize, and empathize with people who are willing to subscribe to your vision for the future and are willing to work with you on that vision . . . I find increasingly that, if I'm able to give a very honest and straightforward perspective to employees on the future and the challenges ahead, it is a great way to get across what I want for the company."

While it is important to pay attention to how Nilekani has been able to inspire others—so important, in fact, that we spend an entire chapter on voice—what makes him an ideal model for this chapter is the fact that before anything else was done he and his partners laid out an image of how things would be made different. That is vision and it is what many leaders have relied on to achieve many a great thing.

•　　•　　•

According to author Jim Collins, Charles Coffin—GE's first president—was the best CEO of all time. Coffin brought to life the vision that a company—as opposed to individual inventors—could systematically innovate and then extract profits from each innovation. To accomplish this, Coffin created America's first research laboratory and introduced the idea of systematic management development. Living at a time of invention, Coffin's vision was GE itself.[19]

The vision took time to come to fruition. The lab was founded in 1900 but did not have its first success until 1907. But the alternative—to rely on outside inventors or a hit-and-miss approach—was too risky and did not provide a sufficiently firm foundation for future growth.

By the time Coffin retired in 1922, after leading the firm for thirty years, GE had 82,000 employees. More important, he created a culture of leadership development that persists to this day. GE today invests about $1 billion annually on training and education programs, and the firm consistently develops some of the best leaders in business.

As the example of Charles Coffin indicates, sometimes a leader's vision takes some time to develop. Other times, however, if a vision is to be realized, it is not patience that one needs but a willingness to adapt. Too often visions fail not because of a lack of commitment or passion but because people are unable to see beyond one way that a vision can come to life.

Certainly there is historical evidence of single-minded leaders realizing their goals and reaping huge rewards. There is no greater example than Henry Ford. Yet, while Ford's stubbornness was an asset in the beginning of his career, taking his company to heights that only he could have ever imagined, it proved a near-fatal flaw later on when his competitors began to provide customers with choices that went far beyond the simple design and color of the Model-T.

While it is true that success can be bred from stubbornness, it is also true that stubbornness leads to vulnerability, which, in time, brings about failure. It is more ideal to be adaptive; it is a quality that marries itself well to the visions of many strong leaders because it helps when a vision is first being realized, and it is essential for surviving challenges.

> Every company begins with a vision, comprised of two wedded elements: a product concept aimed at a particular market and a notion of the way the company needs to be organized to make the most of the market opportunity. Henry Ford did not simply develop a standard car for a mass market, he developed a system of mass production in which, not coincidentally, his own workers might afford the very cars they built. Bill Gates's Microsoft not only designs software for personal computers, the company is its own best evidence that individuals networked by personal computers can be organized into value-adding teams.
>
> —*Harvard Business Review*, 1993 [20]

· · ·

As we said earlier, there are leaders who are visionaries and there are leaders who are not. And then there are people like Tex Schramm, the legendary president of the Dallas Cowboys football team. He is of the former group, but was too generous a man ever to admit it. When we began writing this book, we planned to interview Schramm. Sadly, prior to our speaking with him, he passed away at the age of eighty-three.

One of our colleagues at Russell Reynolds Associates is Joe Bailey, who was senior vice president for Administration with the Dallas Cowboys, where he worked for Schramm for nineteen years. With Bailey's permission, we include here a sizeable portion of the eulogy he delivered at Schramm's funeral. Better than we ever could, it speaks of Schramm's vision and leadership over those many years.

Joe Bailey remembers Tex Schramm

MANY HAVE CALLED him an innovator and that is true. But he was really a visionary in that he knew from the start in 1960 what he wanted his Dallas Cowboys to become and he convinced "his people," as he liked to call us, that the Cowboys could become the most admired and respected franchise in all of sports. Through a multitude of media he positioned us as being "unique"—one of his favorite words. And over the years he successfully created an enduring psychological contract with our fans and the franchise.

He pushed us to do things differently, take risks, and become special. "Dare to be great," he so often said.

And he credited Clint Murchison, owner of the Dallas Cowboys, with providing the platform for that "greatness." His favorite speech, Teddy Roosevelt's "Man in the Arena" was the standard he used to evaluate not only himself but others as well:

> It is not the critic who counts, not the man who points out how the
> strong man stumbles, or where the doer of deeds could have done them
> better. The credit belongs to the man in the arena, whose face is marred
> by dust and sweat and blood, who strives valiantly . . . who knows the
> great enthusiasms, the great devotions; who spends himself in a worthy
> cause, who at the best knows in the end the triumph of high achieve-
> ment, and who at the worst, if he fails, at least fails while daring greatly,
> so that his place shall never be with those cold and timid souls who
> have never known neither victory nor defeat.[21]

Tex, like all great leaders, had the confidence to surround himself with the very strongest—strong in character, strong in dedication to the common goal, and strong in mutual respect. He always said that there are really two types of people: "those who make the organization better" and "those who the organization makes better. Give me as many of the former, and I'll manage around their weaknesses."

For those of us in that latter category, we give him thanks for the opportunity to blossom. For those in the first category, well, they were bountiful and of course, very well remembered.

His philosophy allowed him to assemble some incredibly driven, intelligent, innovative, and often colorful personalities that only a man of Tex's stature and force of personality could keep together all those years.

Tex acknowledged that it was a privilege to be in his position. He would comment, "How lucky I was to have an owner with the right perspective, who believed in hiring the best and letting them do their job, and have some fun along the way," and boy, did we ever have fun. A new franchise, an absolutely great city on the rise with a Texas can-do-anything attitude—the sky was the limit, the stars were aligned, and fortune favored the audaciousness of Tex's leadership.

●　　●　　●

Reading Bailey's words leaves us with a sense of deep respect. His eulogy touched on many of the qualities that made Schramm so effective. And while not all of these qualities were discussed in this chapter, they will be explored in later sections, thus leaving you convinced that Bailey was not just speaking kindly of a friend but describing well an outstanding leader.

Schramm wanted the Cowboys to become the most admired and respected franchise in all of sports. It was a lofty goal, and it alone would merit Schramm's inclusion in this book. However, it was only one of Schramm's visions. For his was not only to create a great sports team, it was also to create a great sport—professional football. And to both, Schramm, like all great leaders, was utterly committed.

When Schramm took the job with the expansion team in Dallas in 1960, he was in a unique position. From an earlier stint with the Los Angeles Rams he was long familiar with the problems facing the sports league with which he was so in love—it was a distant fourth in fan interest, behind baseball, college football and thoroughbred racing. His more recent job at CBS sports, where he produced the first television broadcast of the Winter Olympics, exposed him to the power television had in promoting sports.

Schramm realized that television was the key to professional football's growth. By making the sport more accessible through television, Schramm would be able to accomplish a number of things. First, the fan base of the league would grow exponentially. Second, the reputation of the sport would vastly improve. Third, the revenue that resulted from the television contracts would greatly improve the league's health. Fourth, Schramm's vision for the Dallas Cowboys would be more likely fulfilled.

On the last point, from the first day he stepped into his office, Schramm knew that the fortunes of the Cowboys would only ascend with the league's growth. In fact, it can be argued that by his hand the Dallas Cowboys were the "first carefully calculated, artfully nurtured sports brand."[22] He worked hard to cultivate the team's image, making sure that it was included in the NFL East, where its games would get huge exposure in influential cities like Washington, D.C., and New York.[23]

So, with Commissioner Pete Rozelle, who also thought the league's future depended on television, Schramm worked hard to nurture the NFL's relationships with the major networks. So effective were the two men that in 1964, the NFL signed a two-year agreement with CBS worth $28 million, an increase of 9,200 percent over its 1960 contract.[24]

From this contract was born much of what is important to present-day professional football. Because of it, people no longer saw teams simply as representative of a city but instead as representative of a league. CBS, to justify the cost of the new contract, began airing two games. Viewers began to see more teams from cities other than their own; they became more familiar with more players; they became fans of more teams that were located far away from where they lived. The greatest beneficiary of all of this was of course the team in Dallas—just as Schramm would have designed.

In 1966, Rozelle was looking for a second game to air on Thanksgiving Day, just after Detroit's traditional noon kickoff. There were no takers other than Schramm, who envisioned the game as a good way of increasing the exposure and image of the Cowboys. The game was national; it was aired on a day on which most people would be home, and thus watching television; and the tie-in with Thanksgiving would connect the Cowboys in peoples' minds with all that is good about the holiday.

Schramm's vision for the league and the Cowboys was not just realized on the back of television. He was an innovator like few others before or since. He revolutionized the league by introducing such things as luxury suites, computerized scouting, and a whole slew of game-related rules. He was the originator of an early incarnation of what is now NFL Properties and the mastermind behind the Dallas Cowboys Cheerleaders.

But to vision, there is one thing left to say about Tex Schramm. Like Marshall, he had the gift of foresight. As important as his and Rozelle's vision that television would be the future of the league was Schramm's vision of what the league would turn into if the American Football League and NFL continued to compete against one another. It was Schramm who called Lamar Hunt, founder of the AFL, on April 4, 1966. It was Schramm who Hunt met in a car at Dallas's Love Field to first talk of the merger that would not only connect the two leagues but also be the harbinger of what professional football is today—far and away the most popular sport in America.

•   •   •

In terms of the leadership equation, vision is important because it determines direction. It defines where you are going and where you want to take others. It transcends strategy, but is still grounded in commitment.

In recruiting CEO candidates, we approach vision from several perspectives. One, if the company has a well-established vision that requires nurturing rather than radical reinvention, we look for someone who understands that vision and can speak to what is necessary to kindle the passions of the entire organization to further the vision. In cases where a new or retooled vision might be required, we look for individuals who grasp the essence of the business as it is today but also in terms of what it could become—that's where the ability to dream comes in.

Generally speaking, executives who have the ability to look to the future and imagine what a company, product, service, or business model might evolve into are those who tend to be blessed with "vision." Similarly gifted are those who are good lateral thinkers, able to "connect the dots" between converging trends, opportunities, and competitive threats. Executives who really understand the nitty-gritty of the business and focus on what must be done in the here and now through better blocking and tackling can still be effective leaders, but are likely not a good match for a company that needs some help in the vision department.

Vision, we know, does not properly exist if there is no corresponding action; it is impossible for it to be realized if action is not taken. How that action is inspired, directed, and framed will be the subject of the rest of this book, beginning with the next chapter, voice: the articulation of vision and perhaps the catalyst most critical to its realization.

A perspective from the Russell Reynolds Associates Executive Assessment Team

When compared to other major executive competencies, vision is commonly rated the lowest, executive assessment professionals have found. While vision is often the subject of high-minded conversation in organizations, it is actually elusive and rare.

There is an obvious difference between embracing a vision and creating it, and many leaders, by necessity, are required to embrace a vision that others have developed. This is because only one in ten executives has a propensity for the quality of thinking that is marked by originality and imagination, yet innovative thinking is a basic component of vision.

To be visionary involves two other facets: a breadth of interests, knowledge, and attention—people with this capability cast a wide net as they learn about their business, their markets, the wider business climate, and the world in general; and anticipation, which we sometimes refer to as forward thinking. This literally represents an attempt to see into the future, which is a common fascination for many people. But what is rare is making a prediction and staking one's career on it. Assessment professionals find that "seeing around corners" from executive suites involves risk-taking and boldness, and that many business executives shy away from this challenge.

sources

1. Selected quote, "Vision," http://cybernation.com/victory/quotations/authors/quotes_proverb_japanese.html (accessed February 12, 2004).
2. James C. Collins and Jerry I. Porras, *Built to Last: Successful Habits of Visionary Companies* (New York: HarperBusiness, 1994), p. 97.
3. Jack Welch, with John A. Byrne, *Jack: Straight from the Gut* (New York: Warner Books, 2001), p. 106.
4. Caroline Humer, "IBM's Ex-CEO: No Vision Is Right Vision," *Reuters Business*, November 17, 2002, http://www.reuters.com.
5. Ibid.
6. Wendy Frew, "He's Got the Whole World in His Hands," *Sydney Morning Herald*, April 11, 2003.
7. Cosima Marriner, "Reading Rupert," *Sydney Morning Herald*, October 12, 2002.
8. Stephen Bartholomeusz, "DirecTV Deal Puts Murdoch Within Reach of Global Dream," *The Age*, April 11, 2003.
9. Richard Stenger, "Man on the Moon: Kennedy Speech Ignited the Dream, CNN.com, May 25, 2001, http://www.cnn.com/2001/TECH/space/05/25/kennedy.moon/.
10. Kenneth Labich, "The Seven Keys to Business Leadership, *Fortune*, October 24, 1988.
11. Anders Hallengren, "Nelson Mandela and the Rainbow of Culture," Nobel e-Museum, http://www.nobel.se/peace/articles/mandela/index.html (accessed February 20, 2004).
12. Nelson Mandela, "Nobel Lecture" (acceptance speech for the Nobel Peace Prize, Oslo, Norway, December 10, 1993).
13. Alan Axelrod, *Profiles in Leadership* (New York: Prentice Hall Press, 2003), p. 354.
14. George Marshall, "Commencement Address, Harvard University," keynote address, Cambridge, MA, June 5, 1947, http://www.georgecmarshall.org/lt/speeches/marshall_plan.cfm.
15. Michael J. Hogan, *The Marshall Plan: America, Britain, and the Reconstruction of Western Europe 1947–1952* (Cambridge, UK: Cambridge University Press, 1987).
16. Calculation was based on Indian GAAP (Non-consolidated financials) using financial projections provided by the investment bank UBS Warburg.
17. "Cadence Pips Infy in Best Employer Race: Survey," *The Hindu Business Line*, August 23, 2003.
18. K. Satyamurty, "Infosys named best employer by international consultants." *The Hindu*, June 11, 2002.
19. Jim Collins, "The 10 Greatest CEOs of All Time," *Fortune*, July 21, 2003, p. 68.
20. Roger Martin, "Changing the Mind of the Corporation," *Harvard Business Review*, November–December 1993.
21. Theodore Roosevelt, "The Man in the Arena," speech at the Sorbonne, Paris, France, April 23, 1910, http://www.theodoreroosevelt.org/research/speech%20arena.htm.
22. John Helyar, "Ride 'em Cowboy," *Fortune*, September 29, 2003, p. 59.
23. Ibid.
24. John Maher, "Schramm's Vision Turned NFL into a Sports Goliath," *Austin American-Statesman*, July 16, 2003

3

Voice

There is no index of character so sure as the voice.
—Benjamin Disraeli[1]

The art of communication is the language of leadership.
—James Humes[2]

A VITAL CHALLENGE for every leader is to develop a voice that others not only hear but also wish to follow. This ability is part art, part science and often heavily influenced by the natural gifts a leader possesses.

While the styles of effective communications vary widely, several absolutes are inherent. First, know thy audience, for without this understanding, even brilliant content and style may fail or seem irrelevant. Second, know that trust is essential and cannot be established without integrity and sincerity in motivation, word and deed. Third, consistency of message and frequent repetition are equally essential as are applying the appropriate style and platform. Yes, packaging counts.

We are trained to think that "being smart" matters most, but as Einstein said, "We should take care not to make intellect our god. It has, of course, powerful muscles, but no personality. It cannot lead, it can only serve."

Being right or brilliant is not enough. You may be able to anticipate future events and choose the right vision for your organization, but success depends on how effectively that vision is communicated to others.

Often a leader's success will rest largely on his or her voice. That is, how well they communicate important messages to those they lead and those they need to influence. Without clear, compelling communications, the direction of the enterprise will not be understood and embraced; the role each person plays will be muddied, hampering individual and team effectiveness and the leadership of the company will not be trusted or respected. In short, the odds of failure increase exponentially. Conversely, if a company is led by a strong voice, there is a greater probability of not only meeting but exceeding goals and of the company not simply doing what is possible, but achieving the unimagined.

In 1961, an internal task force concluded that the IBM product line was aging and that the company was susceptible to rivals. As a response, IBM developed System/360, one of the most influential products of the last fifty years. Making computers compatible with one another, System/360 provided customers with more flexibility, becoming the foundation upon which the information age was built.

The questions surrounding the product's release were staggering. First, could there be an adequate return on investment; indeed, could there be any return on investment? IBM had to both hire 60,000 additional workers to man the project and invest $5 billion—roughly three times its revenues—to finance it. And second, would workers and the investment community support System/360? The product would replace all of the company's existing computer lines, including its best seller, the 1401, with a technology the market had never seen. Many people had a vested stake in those older technologies and would be hesitant to dismiss them.[3]

The eventual success of such a monumental product launch was due in large part to the effectiveness of IBM's leadership voice. Despite the challenges, the company's CEO, Thomas J. Watson Jr. was able to convince the investment community that System/360 was a worthwhile undertaking. He was only able to do this by first convincing the IBM workforce.

Watson was effective in his communication to the workers because his message was delivered through the contention system, the platform upon which ideas and products were promoted at IBM. A process that everyone trusted and believed in, the contention system served as Watson's voice when System/360 was still very much in need of workers' support.

Under the contention system, major product decisions at IBM were first made by staff officers, the people who best understood the products and the markets in which they competed, and then by top management. By the time the System/360 proposal reached the Management Review Committee, the final arbiters in the contention system, it had already been checked and balanced against service, engineering, manufacturing, and both the domestic and international marketing divisions.[4] Common ground had been found among all interested parties, most notably the engineers and the marketers, meaning that there were very few hurt feelings and that there was a near consensus as to what the product should do and how it should enter the market.

In a sense, the process had communicated Watson's message, and through the process, he found the support necessary for System/360 to proceed. There was enough energy behind System/360 that Watson was able to present a strong case to the public (i.e., the investment community), justifying the enormous cost required to bring the new product to market.

The voice behind the development of IBM's System/360 was effective for a number of reasons. First, it spoke to the company's continued health, something all audiences cared deeply about. In 1961, IBM felt it needed to make changes if it was to maintain its position of dominance. Second, the message was sincere and truthful. At no time were the challenges of bringing the System/360 to market—the costs and the commitment—avoided. Third, Watson's message was consistent to all audiences and delivered repeatedly to each audience—within IBM and externally to investors. Importantly, the message was being delivered not just by Watson, but also by the IBM choir. By the time Watson made his public pronouncements, the workforce of IBM was already committed to the task at hand due to the extraordinary internal communications process in place. Unique to IBM, the process was not a top-down cascade where senior officers tried convincing the workforce. In fact the reverse was true, with workers justifying the product to management. The consequence of all this was the near universal support of the System/360.

An effective voice requires a combination of public and private interactions. The most moving speech will be futile if it is not backed up with a series of effective conversations with pivotal colleagues. Likewise, if you convince senior executives but fail to connect with the rank and file, your efforts may encounter resistance at every turn.

Business leaders are often confronted by numerous stakeholders whose interests conflict. A management hierarchy is supposed to define responsibility, but, in reality, every organization has informal channels of communication and power that are never accurately captured on paper.

There are ways to cope successfully with such communication challenges, but there is no magic bullet. The leadership of IBM placed their trust in the workforce, thinking that they were the best ones to communicate what was good versus what was bad about the development of the System/360. In other situations, leaders rely on charisma or even a methodology. Some will inspire, others will intimidate. The best, however, are always able to find a reliable means of connecting with the people most vital to their success.

Few leaders have done a better job of finding a "voice" that works than Harry Kraemer, former CEO of Baxter International, Inc. He is listened to because people see in him someone who is sincere and someone they can trust. Kraemer spoke with us and told us that he has built this trust by nurturing a very open work environment where all viewpoints are heard and everyone is treated as he or she would like to be treated.

In his own words: Harry Kraemer

"WHAT DOES DELIVERING the message mean to me as a leader? It pretty much means everything," Kraemer says. "Delivering the message and being the leader involves nonstop communication, making sure that everybody on the team understands what you're trying to do and why.

"The team needs to feel encouraged to ask questions—to challenge you. Because, as a leader, you're not focused on *being* right, you're trying to *do* the right thing, and you must get to the point where the team understands this so that the right thing can be done."

For Kraemer, this is only possible if he follows the Golden Rule: "Making people feel as though they're being treated the way that I'd like to be treated is a constant, nonstop project."

Kraemer devotes a lot of thought to his interactions with employees, as well as with customers and other stakeholders. He asks himself, "What would I want from somebody who is the leader?"

His answer? "I would want them to have self-confidence, but also to have humility.

"Maybe they have more experience than I do; maybe they're lucky and were in the right place at the right time; but they should have their feet on the ground and know that they are no better than anybody else. That person also should be able to be reached.

"Openness, acceptability, and approachability are vital," Kraemer says. To make things happen in a large organization requires not only the right focus, but also a system that facilitates a two-way flow of communication.

Kraemer admits, "I am fortunate to have a voicemail system that connects everybody within our organization around the world. So I can leave messages that 40,000 people can hear, including all the vice presidents, all the directors, you name it. We've got separate distribution with every group, which creates a constantly open environment.

"I probably spend at least four to five hours a day on voicemail. The constancy and consistency are absolutely crucial. Through our 'Ask Harry' function, anyone who has a question can send me an email or voicemail and know they'll get an answer.

"I also write a monthly summary called the "CEO Update" in *Baxter Today*, in which I talk about what's going well and what isn't. Ten years ago, when I first started writing the updates, I didn't realize how they'd develop. I just began working in some humorous stories about my children called 'On the Homefront.' And then, when I'd visit the facilities, people would talk about a piece I wrote, and it was clear that they were relating to me as a person because of the family stories." Kraemer discovered that just by being himself, he made it easier for his employees to connect with him, which in turn made it easier for them to accept his messages and voice.

Kraemer also attributes his manner with people today to his childhood. "My dad was a salesman, and we moved almost every year when I was a kid," he recalls. "For me, the impact of that was to always be thinking, 'I don't know how long I'm going to be here, so I'm going to get to know people quickly.' The whole idea that I'm going to be as open as I can and get around as quick as I can has always been important to me. I'm really going to make sure that I make contact with everybody."

●　　●　　●

In Harry Kraemer, there are two qualities that typify many successful leaders: a desire to reach out to people and a deep reservoir of energy. His leadership voice is so successful because of the constant efforts he makes to get people to recognize him as someone to whom they can relate, as someone who always keeps their best interests in mind. Further, he does not pretend that he has all the answers. Like IBM's Watson, he puts trust in the dialogue of his company's labor force. By making sure that his employees have a sense of who he is and involving others in the decision-making process, Kraemer builds their trust in him and strengthens the employees' ties to the company.

You can be the most compelling speaker in the world, but still fail because you are insincere and have not earned the trust of others. History presents innumerable examples of public confidence eroding due to a disconnect between a leader's words and his or her actions.

In 2002, Russell Reynolds Associates commissioned a survey of nearly four hundred institutional investors from six countries: China, France, Germany, Japan, the United Kingdom, and the United States. According to the survey, the single most important factor investors considered when making investment decisions was the "integrity of the information provided by the company," with more than nine in 10 investors giving this factor the greatest weight. [5]

But there was a credibility gap where it mattered most. Investors in all six nations did not feel comfortable with the credibility of available information. In fact, in every nation surveyed except the United States, fewer than half the investors found the available information to be credible; in the United States, just more than half of found it to be so.

Similarly disturbing, only 43 percent of the investors surveyed felt that the information they received from direct meetings with CEOs was credible. One may argue that this lack of credibility is a function of today's business environment. In a sense, it does not matter because the impact is the same: a lack of trust from the audience hampers the relationship.

This is not just an ethical issue. Lack of trust exacts a heavy price on a leader's business. Negotiations take longer. Stakeholders look longer for alternatives. Waste grows as other parties seek out ways to protect themselves. Key talents find employment elsewhere. Morale is lower. Things get done improperly or sometimes not at all.

In their book *Credibility*, authors James Kouzes and Barry Posner argue:

> To earn and strengthen leadership credibility, leaders must do what we say we will do....
>
> That "we" is crucial . . . certainly leaders are expected to keep their promises and follow through on their commitments. But what they say also must be what we, the constituents, believe. To take people to places they have never been before, leaders and constituents must be on the same path.[6]

The authors conclude their argument with the reminder that "leadership, after all, exists only in the eyes of the constituents." We interpret this to mean that even the greatest raw talent can be wasted if a leader fails to earn the trust and respect of others.

To better illustrate this point, let us return to the example of Dallas Cowboys president Tex Schramm and his influence in bringing about the merger between the NFL and the AFL. After several weeks of discussion, Schramm and AFL founder, Lamar Hunt, had come to some agreement regarding how the merger should take place and, to a certain degree, what the new league would look like. They were ready to move toward completion when, out of nowhere, the NFL's New York Giants signed Pete Gogolak away from the AFL's Buffalo Bills. The signing, to say the least, immediately complicated the negotiations. Many of the AFL owners became skeptical that Schramm and the NFL were not negotiating in good faith and could not be trusted to go forward with the merger.[7]

Because the New York Giants acted in a way that contradicted Schramm's message to the AFL, the Cowboys president's leadership position faltered and the credibility of the negotiation was brought into question. The two leagues would not have merged if that question of credibility remained, and professional football in the United States would look very different than it does today. Schramm was able to dissipate the rival league's fears by again speaking to Hunt and assuring him that the negotiation was being conducted in a fair way and that the Giants' actions were as much a surprise to him as they were to Hunt.

From this example, we hope to illustrate how precious and tenuous trust actually is. Trust exists only as a result of much hard work and can disappear overnight if actions contradict the message. It requires constant nurturing. Voice is about much more than words and delivery style. It is about consistency, sincerity, commitment, tenacity, and perhaps above all, respect for others.

Klaus Kleinfeld, member of the Corporate Executive Committee at Siemens AG, speaks well on the subject of trust and respect:

"I have a general respect for every individual, even if I don't know them personally. I've seen in my life that if I'd had the opportunity to talk to a person long enough, there's always something that I've found totally fascinating . . . no matter from which area of life that individual may have come.

"You must demonstrate that respect, even while you may need to be tough on certain issues. And I don't think that those two elements oppose each other. In fact, they go together because they create a totally candid relationship. Most people are smart enough to see when you are not candid. And when you're not candid, you cannot build a relationship because there is a missing element of trust. For me, trust is critical, not only in the personal relationships, but also in organizational relationships. It is absolutely essential."

●　　●　　●

There are many reasons to communicate, but for our current purposes there are only two. First is the need to impart information. A leader builds trust, cohesiveness, and strong performance by quite simply keeping people "in the loop." This doesn't simply refer to giving people the information they need to do their jobs; it means making them feel included as part of the team, and creating trust that in turn leads them to trust the leader. And while the content is very important, so is the tone of the delivery mechanism.

Second, a leader must also motivate, to convince the audience to believe in his or her vision, to get them to move from where they are now to a place they may or may not imagine or seek. As a motivational tool, effective voice is far from common, but then it is also far more memorable. For when a voice truly motivates, then vision, commitment, and passion are passed from one person or group to the next and people are able to do great things.

Whether the intention is to inform or motivate, the leader must deliver the message in a way that resonates with the audience's personal priorities. The speech British prime minister Winston Churchill gave before the House of Commons on June 18, 1940, is a classic example of how achieving this connection can exact heretofore unimaginable will and determination. Here is the final passage of that speech:

> What General Weygand called the Battle of France is over. I expect that the Battle of Britain is about to begin. Upon this battle depends the survival of Christian civilization. Upon it depends our own British life, and the long continuity of our institutions and our Empire. The whole fury and might of the enemy must very soon be turned on us. Hitler knows that he will have to break us in this Island or lose the war. If we can stand up to him, all Europe may be free and the life of the world may move forward into broad, sunlit uplands. But if we fail, then the whole world, including the United States, including all that we have known and cared for, will sink into the abyss of a new Dark Age made more sinister, and perhaps more protracted, by the lights of perverted science. Let us therefore brace ourselves to our duties, and so bear ourselves that, if the British Empire and its Commonwealth last for a thousand years, men will still say, "This was their finest hour." [8]

Churchill's message resonated for a number of reasons, but, most importantly, he captured the attention of his audience completely because he so artfully articulated what every person in that room cared about—their pride, the future of the country, and the future of Europe.

After the fall of France, many in England felt defeated, quickly acquiring a sense of resignation. Churchill's objective was to make sure that that feeling did not become overwhelming. In countless speeches, he reminded the British people that they still held the sword in their hands and that they would still use it. In his words there existed not just the notion that England could fight Germany, but would fight and be victorious over Germany.

In addition to its speaking of things the audience cared about, Churchill's voice had impact for a reason not yet touched upon in our discussion—the use of language to better deliver a point.

In light of the circumstances, it was not enough that Churchill just ask to be followed. The horrors put upon Britain during the course of the pending Battle of Britain would be so great that no person could suffer through them on mere words. Churchill knew that if Britain were to remain independent, then his voice would have to rise up and meet the challenge that Germany posed to that independence.

To do that, Churchill was very selective in his word choice, making sure to put the battle in the most significant of historical contexts. By tying their fates to destiny, Churchill felt he could secure the resolve of his compatriots. He deliberately cast the British in the roles of saviors, as the soldiers of God, the worthy successors of all ancient people put upon by the horrors of tyranny. Since many of his countrymen were not Christian, such wording was bold. But nevertheless, Churchill's choices were smart. He knew that if Britain was going to survive, it would need God, so he reminded the British that God was also in need of them.[9] Churchill was not ignorant of the machinations of Nazi Germany and what was left in the wake of the blitzkrieg. The British, by fighting on, would not only aid in stopping a turning tide, but would also give hope to the pockets of resistance in occupied countries, standing as a lasting example of humanity.

By delivery and word choice, Churchill was able to obtain his most desired results. What words a leader uses can dictate how resonant the message will be, thus influencing the power of his or her voice.

It is not always appropriate for a message to sound as if it is coming from a showman. Abraham Lincoln, the sixteenth president of the United States and another great communicator, understood this when he said, "What kills a skunk is the publicity it gives itself."[10] What voice a leader uses, what words he or she chooses, needs to reflect properly on the current circumstances and the audience being addressed. The times dictated that Churchill lift his voice to the grandest scale, as only then would attention be paid to him. In another situation, under entirely different circumstances, such wording could be seen as inappropriate and summarily dismissed. For example, would it make sense for a leader to reference the "destiny of man" if the message being delivered had to do with a company becoming more efficient and streamlined?

What might be more appropriate to a business setting—when an emotional response is needed to motivate others to do their best work—is for a leader's message to be packaged in a story. Stories, by bringing facts to life, connect people, generating the type of emotional response that will drive them to action.

Henri de Castries, chairman of the Management Board and chief executive officer of AXA, often chooses to reference stories and anecdotes as a means of motivating the troops. Talking to us of a challenge faced by the company a few years ago, de Castries offers evidence as to how effective a story can be in motivating people.

In his own words: Henri de Castries

"I WAS TRYING to get us to better capture the evolution of the business. To do that, I thought what we needed to do was look beyond a historical perspective, which, I think, can be very confining.

"For us, that meant thinking of insurance in broader terms. I wanted the people who worked with me to think that what we were doing was broader than the traditional definition of insurance. I didn't want them to think of the industry as being as broad as financial services. But I wanted them to move in that direction toward something I called, and has now come to be known as, financial protection.

"How I motivated people to make this jump, to get them to think about their jobs and the company in a new way was, in truth, quite simple. In communicating my message, I would refer to other industries with which they were already quite familiar, pointing out that what I was asking them to do had already been done to great effect elsewhere.

"I took as my example the transport industry, suggesting that what we were doing was similar to the transition that industry underwent at the end of the nineteenth century. So many businesses at the time thought that the industry's growth was dependent on the making of better carriages. But, in fact, the companies that did well were not at all concerned with carriages. Their focus was to look beyond the traditional interpretation of the industry. To them, the industry was not about carriages but about getting people from point A to point B. Their intent then was both to speed up and make easier the process of moving between these two points.

"I wanted us to think of what we were trying to do in those terms. This story brought it home for a number of people. It illustrated very well what we were trying to accomplish and made it easier for people to put their arms around what we were trying to become."

> The newest computer can merely compound, at speed, the oldest problem in the relations between human beings, and in the end the communicator will be confronted with the old problem, of what to say and how to say it.
>
> —Edward R. Murrow[11]

Thus, de Castries was better able to motivate people by packaging his message into a story. By making reference to the history of the transport industry, he provided people with two different scenarios, both of which were easily understood. The first was that if people could embrace the concept of financial protection then AXA would grow and prosper, much as those companies did that reinterpreted the definition of the transportation industry. The second was that if people did not embrace this new idea of what insurance could be, than AXA's fate would be no different than that of those who held strongly to the belief that the transportation industry's growth would be the result of changes made to the carriage, not the reimagining of what the carriage represented.

•   •   •

Former U.S. president Ronald Reagan was renowned as a "storyteller." Often when trying to get the American people to commit to an idea, he made what he was saying more reasonable and palatable by humanizing it, articulating goals in terms that were imminently relatable to his audience. The best examples of Reagan's effective storytelling are his addresses to the American people.

The following is an excerpt from Reagan's first inaugural address, dated January 20, 1981. Notice how he encourages people to make the changes necessary to the country's future by appealing to their connection to someone like themselves.

> This is the first time in history that this ceremony has been held, as you have been told, on this West Front of the Capitol. Standing here, one faces a magnificent vista, opening up on this city's special beauty and history. At the end of this open mall are those shrines to the giants on whose shoulders we stand . . .

Beyond those monuments to heroism is the Potomac River, and on the far shore the sloping hills of Arlington National Cemetery with its row on row of simple white markers bearing crosses or Stars of David. They add up to only a tiny fraction of the price that has been paid for our freedom.

Each one of those markers is a monument to the kinds of hero I spoke of earlier. Their lives ended in places called Belleau Wood, The Argonne, Omaha Beach, Salerno and halfway around the world on Guadalcanal, Tarawa, Pork Chop Hill, the Chosin Reservoir, and in a hundred rice paddies and jungles of a place called Vietnam.

Under one such marker lies a young man—Martin Treptow—who left his job in a small town barber shop in 1917 to go to France with the famed Rainbow Division. There, on the western front, he was killed trying to carry a message between battalions under heavy artillery fire.

We are told that on his body was found a diary. On the flyleaf under the heading, "My Pledge," he had written these words: "America must win this war. Therefore, I will work, I will save, I will sacrifice, I will endure, I will fight cheerfully and do my utmost, as if the issue of the whole struggle depended on me alone."

The crisis we are facing today does not require of us the kind of sacrifice that Martin Treptow and so many thousands of others were called upon to make. It does require, however, our best effort, and our willingness to believe in ourselves and to believe in our capacity to perform great deeds; to believe that together, with God's help, we can and will resolve the problems which now confront us.[12]

Again, by relating what was required of the country to images and feelings with which each person in his audience was familiar, Reagan made it easier for people to attach and commit themselves to those goals he had set out to achieve during the first years of his presidency.

Sometimes it is not enough for leaders to share a story so that others can be motivated. Instead, they provide their team with an experience that they can share with others. De Castries told us that he once took his 250 top executives to the Amazon basin for a team-building retreat, where he had them cross a piranha-infested river. As far as we know, all survived to repeat the tale.

Aside from helping to gain initial support, how a leader chooses to deliver a message can also go a long way in quashing criticism. The late-nineteenth-century German industrialist August Thyssen performed a masterstroke, one that quite possibly saved his growing empire, when he challenged those critical of him to back their words with action.

Trying to create cost advantages through vertical integration, Thyssen had built a massive steel plant in Alsace-Lorraine. Immediately, he met with criticism from the financial press who questioned his ability not only to pay for the project but also for the vision he had for his company. Thyssen's response was both simple and dramatic. He placed an advertisement in a well-known trade magazine, inviting any creditors who felt anxious about his finances to meet him in Mulheim (his company's headquarters) where they would receive payment in full. [13]

Thyssen's message became stronger as result of his answering the press's questions with a challenge. He showed that he believed in himself and his company. The result was that his vision of growth through expansion became more convincing; his voice became more effective after he overcame his critics.

•   •   •

No matter how effectively a leader might deliver a message once, the communications challenge has just begun. Particularly in today's world where we all are bombarded with input, data, impressions, points of view and other emotional stimuli, we learn and are motivated by repetition.

In fact, it was through our conversation with William Wrigley Jr. chairman and CEO of the Wm. Wrigley Jr. Company, that we learned of how pervasive a message must be in order for people to take stock in it. He speaks of how he was able to introduce the company to a set of new corporate principles:

"We distributed the information, but went beyond just doing the traditional stuff. We conducted live feeds to seventeen markets around the world, highlighting the strategic plan. The principles were a part of that. It was a very big deal technologically, and it also had a huge impact.

"The senior executive team had also done multiple world tours. Back in 2000 we flew the entire leadership team around the world. In nine days we went to eighteen locations, having town hall meetings and answering whatever questions people had. We've continued to reinforce these values in all of our communications. In addition, we've begun to measure people's performance in part by how well they've embraced these values that we think are so important."

50

If you want people to take hold of a message, it is not enough to say it only once because there are too many other stimuli competing for people's attention. The founder and CEO of FedEx, Fred Smith, like Wrigley, sees repetition as very important to the buy-in of a firm's strategy. "Once senior management has bought into a refined strategy, we then communicate that strategy in every way we can think of," he says. "We put it in the mission statement and into the employee handbooks. We tie our business plans and our incentive plans to it. We have one of the biggest industrial TV networks in the world, and we use it to make sure our employees understand what we're trying to do and why we're trying to do it."[14]

The key to both Wrigley's and Smith's approaches is in their breadth and depth. Both of their companies are connecting the way people get paid with the goals of the firm. While this sounds like an obvious step, time and again new initiatives fail because leaders tell their employees to do one thing, but pay them to do another. By rewarding the behavior that he is encouraging, Smith and Wrigley are actively telling their employees that it is in their best interest to listen to what is being communicated.

Repeating a message is often necessary if people are going to embrace it. But repetition can also help the speaker better define what he or she is trying to say. Once former Chairman and CEO Jack Welch committed General Electric to the notion that the company would be either number one or number two in all of the businesses in which it competed, he made sure that that message was repeated so often that it would inform the work-related decisions of every person working at the company.

But as he communicated that message to other people, Welch was also better able to define it, so that those he was talking to could more quickly grasp what he was trying to accomplish. Interestingly enough, it was while he was speaking with his wife over dinner that he was able to come up with the clearest expression of what he was trying to say.

Taking out a napkin, Welch drew three circles and divided the company's businesses into one of three sectors: core manufacturing, technology, and services. Any business outside of one those circles would either be fixed, sold, or closed. Over the next couple of weeks he worked on the chart with his team, filling in whatever details he might have missed. In the end, Welch thought they had a product that really hit the mark. It was the simple theoretical tool he had sought to explain his strategy, and it would better help people implement the new ambition of GE being number one or number two in all of the businesses in which it competed. Welch began using it everywhere, turning it into such a point of focus that in 1984 *Forbes* magazine featured it in a cover story on GE.[15]

* * *

One of our goals in writing this book was to show how universal are the leadership traits being discussed and how they have persisted throughout history. In the case of voice, this also applies to knowing how to choose the appropriate venue or platform for your communications.

In ancient Greece, the Olympics, like the other great international festivals, drew vast audiences, composed mostly of people from the upper classes. It was a venue at which aristocrats could speak and connect with their social peers from other states. Here is where political and business proposals were made, as the audience was powerful enough to bring good ideas to motion.

None of this was lost on Herodotus, considered the father of history. How he used the Olympics as a means of realizing his professional goals is described well by Lucian, an author from the second century:

> [Traveling from Asia Minor] Herodotus considered how both he and his writings might become notable and renowned as quickly as possible and in the most trouble-free manner [since visits to various cities would involve delay]. . . .Therefore, he decided not to disperse his effort nor to gather and collect a public response by audience segments little by little. But he planned (if it might be possible) to win all the Greeks together somewhere [so he presented his work at the Olympic Games]. . . . Immediately everyone knew of him better than even the Olympic victors themselves. And there was no one who had not heard the name of Herodotus, some hearing him themselves at Olympia and the rest learning from those returning from the festival. And if he showed up anywhere, people pointed him out.[16]

Herodotus knew his audience to be such that, if he spoke well, his goals would be met; he would be known throughout Greece. The attendants of the games were leaders of their respective societies. They were the ones others listened to and admired. By impressing them, Herodotus was able to make an impression on all of Greece as they relayed his message to others upon their return home.

Gaining access to a platform that allows a voice to reach the right audience remains as much a challenge now as it was in ancient times. When he was trying to build the brand identity of IBM, Thomas Watson Sr., who headed the company prior to his son, was not able to reach his desired audience—the decision makers of large institutions—through conventional means. Neither he nor his company were noteworthy enough to attract much attention from the press, which at the time was the most direct way for a business leader to gain access to large numbers of people. Unfazed, Watson set out on another path. He sent the company's newsletter, *Think*, to every person whose support he thought might be useful to IBM's growth, including the presidents of all colleges in the United States and every member of the U.S. Congress.[17] By recognizing which audience was most important to his goals, Watson overcame the obstacle of his low profile and found a platform from which he could deliver his message successfully.

Equally creative in his approach to reaching an audience is Lloyd's of London chairman Lord Peter Levene, who led the rebuilding of Canary Wharf, the business district not far from the heart of London. As he relayed to us the story of how he drove people to the development, we were reminded of how varied communication platforms can be and of how important they are to the effectiveness of a leader's voice.

In his own words: Lord Peter Levene

"WHEN I GOT to Canary Wharf, I spent the first two or three months looking around the place, trying to find out what was wrong with it. I only found one thing. Nobody had the same perspective and they didn't believe the things we were saying. So the most immediate challenge, and in my mind it was a large one, was to persuade a very skeptical public that the place was in good shape. And that took two years.

"We did all sorts of extraordinary things. We took out advertisements and placed them in subways. We ran competitions where the winners were invited to visit the place. I think that was quite effective in educating people about what was happening here.

"On top of that, I did something which I've also done here at Lloyd's. I had regular lunches, almost every week, with the "great and the good." I made a real effort to try to get them down there to look over the place.

"When I started, I'd phone up the chairmen and CEOs of major companies whom I knew, and I'd say, 'Hey, you know, I'm at Canary Wharf now. Come down and have a look at it.'

"And they'd all say, 'Well . . .'

"And I'd say, 'Well, do you know where it is?' And certainly in those days, they'd say, 'Well, not exactly.'

"And I'd nag them until they came and each time, the same thing happened. They'd turn up a half an hour early for lunch—because, you see, it was a lot closer than they had imagined. Their eyes were opened.

"Then, after lunch, when I showed them around the thing, they started saying, 'This place is amazing.'

"After a few months, the desired result unfolded. I would bump into other acquaintances and they would say to me, 'Oh, you had old Joe down there for lunch the other day. He told me it was absolutely amazing. Can I come down and see it?'

"Of course, as soon as that happened, I knew we were starting to win."

Levene's message was simple. He wanted to apprise people of the value and quality of Canary Wharf. By using platforms appropriate to his two audiences, he was successful in communicating that message and motivating people to take an interest in the property. By taking out advertisements and running competitions, Levene used the platform of publicity to inform the people who would visit the area of what was going on at Canary Wharf. By inviting business leaders to lunch and showing them how accessible and attractive Canary Wharf was, Levene used the more intimate platform of conversation—as well as the venue itself—to build the interest of potential tenants in the complex's commercial spaces.

●　　●　　●

Many leaders have enormous and diverse audiences to reach. From investors to customers to regulators to competitors, the logistics of communicating can be mind-boggling. These days, the media is most often viewed as the conduit to the masses as well as highly targeted audiences. Love it or hate it, communicating via the media is almost always de rigueur for leaders in all parts of the world, be it editorial or advertising, print, broadcast, electronic or other means.

Few people took better advantage of the press than Henry Ford. During the 1920s, he and the Ford Motor Company were the subjects of more magazine articles than the combined total of the next ten most publicized corporations.[18] Envisioning universal car ownership, he shamelessly used the press to reach the audience—the buying public—who would bring his goal to fruition.

Ford saw in the nascent auto industry a very competitive market. If he was going to succeed, he was going to have to make his cars more attractive than his competitors' products. He did this in a way that is now long familiar. He introduced mass production to the auto industry. By doing this, he lowered his costs and increased his output, resulting in lower selling prices. Ford then made cars affordable to the masses.

Price, however, was not something that Ford could compete on forever. He saw mass production as being essential to the development of industry and promoted it as such. Much of what has been written about Ford concerns his influence on the practices of industry.

Ford's genius, however, did not exist only in manufacturing; it was also in his voice. He used the press to communicate his vision that every person should own a car, ideally one made by the Ford Motor Company. Part of that communication was in his message of how he enabled people to own and enjoy cars. Thus, in most of the articles in which Ford was the subject, space would inevitably be devoted to the fact that he increased worker wages to five dollars a day, reduced the average workday from ten to nine hours, and changed the average workweek from six to five days. The articles about Ford showed how the Ford Motor Company was promoting consumer buying power through higher wages and endorsing people to take more time out for leisure.[19]

By articulating his message in such a way, Ford used his voice to increase his competitive advantage. He was successful because of his recognition of the appropriate audience and the platform by which he could most effectively reach that audience. Reading and hearing about the implementations made by Ford resulted in his being lionized by the public. Many thought of him as the equal of Columbus and Moses.[20] People bought his product because of who they imagined Ford to be, and it was this goodwill that enabled the Ford Motor Company to survive in later years, during the ascent of General Motors.

Many seasoned leaders may view Ford's success with the media as an anachronism.. We would not attempt to take on a critique of dealing with the modern media in this effort, except to say that the precepts that apply to having an effective voice discussed within this chapter all apply to dealing effectively with the media, beginning with trust-based communications.

The backlash against the credibility of corporate executives we've seen in recent years is not frivolous. While it may seem as though the sins of a few are attributed to many, the critical coverage business leaders have received stems in part from a disconnect between what business leaders say and what they actually do. The media will remain a primary conduit between business and its audiences; thus, it is to the benefit of many leaders to view it not as a pariah that can easily be manipulated but as a tool useful in making well known all things important.

•   •   •

You might think that an effective voice would be the easiest of all leadership traits to recognize and evaluate. On one hand, yes, it is. Certainly where energy, articulation, expressiveness, and style are concerned, individuals are demonstrating their communications skills during any interaction. But as we have pointed out, voice is more than speaking well. Leaders with voice also understand the realm of communication—how to communicate what, through which mechanism when. Recognizing that talent is a bit trickier. Similarly, not all effective speakers are energetic and expressive. Some connect with their audiences because of their sincerity and credibility, for example.

In fact, it is easy at times to be fooled by the slick communicator. Too much polish on the exterior can sometimes mask a rather empty interior— something that eventually will be exposed. Our research suggests that people with strong voices have often shown strong leadership skills from a very early age. Look at the track record of the very slick communicator carefully to see what substance and results flow from the well-packaged delivery.

We also pay close attention to how candidates speak to us. Most individuals who speak deliberately, who pause to allow for interaction, will carry this very important leadership trait, because when a person gives others the chance to absorb and respond to a message, he or she is enabling others to become motivated.

Too many of us think that a strong voice is only something given at birth—you either have it or you do not. And while it is true that some leaders come naturally to their roles as communicators, a strong voice is something that can be learned and improved upon. Many executives have been "media trained" or "presentation trained." The techniques used by quality trainers can make enormous improvements in a speaker's effectiveness—not by changing the person fundamentally but by helping that individual to make the most out of the natural communications gifts he or she has. What many do not appreciate is that working on delivery is a lifelong journey. One training session does not an orator make. Leaders who appreciate how very important their voices are to their success will work on the communications skills throughout their careers.

A perspective from the Russell Reynolds Associates Executive Assessment Team

When it comes to delivering leadership messages, CEOs and other upper-level executives can have a tendency to rush ahead of their organizations, forgetting to bring them along for the ride.

A CEO often has had previous success in his or her career because of their drive, energy, and quickness. This "push" factor has helped them run around and through roadblocks. It's also helped them get noticed and promoted through middle management. This unique and efficient ability to diagnose a problem or situation and determine a solution is a strength that has brought them rewards throughout their careers. Yet many executives move forward with impatience, emotion, and speed. They end up standing at the top of a hill, planting a flag. When they look around them, the members of the organization are back on the previous hill, scratching their heads. When leaders are asked about this after the fact, they often state that they were "too busy to communicate" or that they were "absorbed in their thinking and analysis."

In such circumstances, the executives have made at least one of four classic, crucial mistakes:

1. They may not have been as clear and specific as they thought, and none of the people reporting directly to them had the temerity to ask for more clarity and understanding.
2. They may have changed the goal, thinking that there was clarity about the change, when in fact there was not.
3. They failed to relate a change or new ideas back to the original goal. In these situations, members of the team may feel that they have conflicting and confusing goals and may perceive that there is not a steady hand at the helm.
4. They did not monitor the progress of the directors of the team.

Excellent leaders know, with amazing subtlety, where each member of their team is in their progress toward the agreed upon objectives. These effective leaders understand how the objectives match the unique goals and interests of every team member and how each person is feeling about their progress. This phenomenon of "isolated acceleration" also occurs with boards of directors, when CEOs may believe they have the buy-in of their boards when, in fact, they do not. This leads a CEO to act in isolation. On some occasions, the board needs a strong set of binoculars to find the CEO; the CEO may even have accelerated to an end point that is unacceptable to the board. This is a classic cause for a CEO's departure.

sources

1. Selected quote, "Voice," http://www.brainyquote.com/quotes/authors/b/benjamin_disraeli.html (accessed February 13, 2004).

2. Selected quote, "Voice," http://www.cyber-nation.com/victory/quotations/subjects/quotes_communication.html (accessed February 13, 2004).

3. Rowena Olegario, "IBM and the Two Thomas J. Watsons," in *Creating Modern Capitalism: How Entrepreneurs Companies, and Countries Triumphed in Three Industrial Revolutions*, ed. Thomas K. McCraw, (Cambridge, MA: Harvard University Press, 1997), p. 367.

4. Ibid., p. 385.

5. *Formula for Confidence: Resetting the Investment Criteria after the Boom and Bust*, Corporate Communications (New York: Russell Reynolds Associates, 2003).

6. James M. Kouzes and Barry Z. Posner, *Credibility: How Leaders Gain and Lose It, Why People Demand It* (San Francisco: Jossey-Bass, 2003).

7. Rick Gosselin, "Schramm a Pivotal Figure in Changing NFL Landscape," *Dallas Morning News*, July 16, 2003.

8. Winston Churchill, "Their Finest Hour," speech to the House of Commons, London, June 18, 1940, http://www.winstonchurchill.org/i4a/pages/index.cfm?pageid=418.

9. Dan Johnson, "The Battle of Britain," June 2000, http://members.fortunecity.co.uk/uk1/battle.htm (accessed December 20, 2003).

10. Selected quote, "Voice," http://www.brainyquote.com/quotes/quotes/a/abrahamlin103270.html (accessed March 9, 2004).

11. Selected quote, "Voice," http://www.bartleby.com/63/15/8415.html (accessed February 13, 2004).

12. Ronald Reagan, "1st Inaugural Address," speech on the West Portico of the Capitol, Washington, D.C., January 20, 1981, http://www.thisnation.com/library/inaugural/reagan1.html.

13. Jeffrey Fear, "August Thyssen and German Steel," in *Creating Modern Capitalism*, p. 197.

14. "How to Keep Your Company's Edge," *Business* 2.0, December 1, 2003.

15. Ibid., p. 110.

16. Thomas J. Figueira, T. Corey Brennan, and Rachel Hall Sternberg, *Wisdom from the Ancients: Enduring Business Lessons from Alexander the Great, Julius Caesar, and the Illustrious Leaders of Ancient Greece and Rome*, ed. Julia Heskel (Cambridge, MA: Perseus Publishing, 2001), p. 40.

17. Olegario, " IBM and the Two Thomas Watsons," p. 357.

18. Thomas K. McCraw and Richard S. Tedlow, "Henry Ford, Alfred Sloan, and the Three Phases of Marketing," in *Creating Modern Capitalism*, p. 275.

19. Ibid.

20. Ibid.

4

Heart

At the heart of any good business is a chief executive officer with one.
—Malcolm Forbes[1]

Civilizations proceed from the heart rather than from the head.
—Mark Twain[2]

MANY LEADERS WANT to feel that their work is meaningful, that it either helps others, impacts a larger community or improves the quality of life for all mankind. Living a meaningful life appeals to their sense of humanity.

We refer to this sense of humanity as "having a heart." A leader who shows heart is better able to connect with others—people want to help him or her achieve a goal in response to a generous display of caring.

Heart, unlike some other leadership traits, cannot be taught but must come from within oneself. Leaders with heart inspire others to do great things through their example.

As a trait, heart can take on many forms. Some leaders demonstrate it through an incredible work ethic or by creating energy wherever they go. Others display it through compassion. And then there are those whose heart is shown as they embrace goals that go far beyond the bottom line.

Mexico City, 1968 Olympic Games—Few were left to see the lone, broken runner come into the stadium. His leg was bloodied, wrapped in a loose-fitting bandage. The winner of the marathon had been declared over an hour earlier. But it was not for a medal that Tanzania's John Stephen Akhwari raced; he was pursuing a far greater goal. For those lucky enough to see him finish, there was no bitter bite to the cold night's air. There was, instead, the proud sense of awe that comes with the realization that the heart of man is both beautiful and truly difficult to break.

When asked by a reporter why he had not given up when there was no chance of winning, Akhwari stood for moment, a bit confused. Finally, he answered, "My country did not send me five thousand miles to start the race, they sent me five thousand miles to finish." [3]

Sometimes in life, the greatest rewards do not go to the victors, but instead to the defeated. For it is in the eyes of the defeated that we often see ourselves. John Stephen Akhwari shows us by his example that people can be strong of will and also of character. He is evidence that heart enables one to do the seemingly impossible. For that we reward him not with a medal, but with our admiration and the belief that, in some ways, he is a leader.

He wanted others to view Tanzania with respect. He did not want people to think that Tanzanians were quitters, so he worked harder as the running became more and more painful, keeping his focus on finishing the race. More than any victor's, his was clearly the Olympian feat—a display of heart that inspired people around the world.

People still want to follow the example of John Stephen Akhwari. His words give voice to our struggles, driving us forward. Akhwari remains a person from whom we can all learn, because we find in him that which will motivate us in our own journeys—heart.

• • •

Theodore Roosevelt, the twenty-sixth president of the United States, wrote the preface to a biography of the black educator Booker T. Washington, in which he said of Washington, "He did justice to every man. He did justice to those to whom it was a hard thing to do justice. He showed mercy; and this meant that he showed mercy not only to the poor, and to those beneath him, but that he showed mercy by an understanding of the shortcomings of those who failed to do him justice, and failed to do his race justice." [4]

Born a slave in 1856, Washington surmounted almost inconceivable obstacles to get an education and never lost his passion for educating newly freed African-Americans. In 1881 he founded Tuskegee Normal and Industrial Institute. He dedicated his life to educating others and serving as a bridge between blacks and whites during the painful and difficult days after emancipation.

A talented public speaker, Washington often turned down lucrative offers to speak, dedicating himself instead to the building and nurturing of the Tuskegee Institute. However, when he did speak, or talked of public speaking, he revealed a bit of his character and what made him such a strong leader.

"I believe," said Washington, "that one always does himself and his audience an injustice when he speaks merely for the sake of speaking.

"I do not believe that one should speak unless, deep down in his heart, he feels convinced that he has a message to deliver. When one feels, from the bottom of his feet to the top of his head, that he has something to say that is going to help some individual or some cause, then let him say it; and in delivering his message . . . [nothing] can take the place of *soul* in an address. When I have an address to deliver, I like to forget all about the rules for the proper use of the English language, and all about rhetoric and that sort of thing, and I like to make the audience forget all about these things, too." [5]

Heart is what makes a man like Washington travel five hundred miles without resources or supporters or even a sense of what lies ahead, so that he can plead for the chance for others to be educated. It is a trait that goes beyond perseverance and backbone, which we will address later in the book. It is a passion to live your life with conviction and to reach out and help people.

●　　●　　●

A leader with heart informs others of his or her humanity. Such a person is not just concerned with the bottom line, but is also sympathetic to the needs and wants of others. Because of his or her desire to help others, workers are more apt to connect to and follow the example of a leader who displays this trait.

Heart is something that a leader shows not only through words, but also through actions. We have already seen examples of it. Churchill's heart made him a more effective communicator as he inspired Britain to stand up and continue its fight against Germany. Heart can drive a remarkable work ethic since it underlies compassion for others, and it permits many to see beyond the bottom line. In this chapter, we examine various ways in which heart presents itself, enabling leaders to push others to achieve great deeds.

We have said that the traits discussed in this book are universal, appearing throughout history, across industries and professions. Leadership qualities are not exclusive to the worlds of business, politics, or the military. Leadership can be found wherever people are bound by a common interest or need. In that sense, heart is the purest leadership quality, and we can learn much from observing this dynamic all around us—in the community or classroom, for a cause or competition, on behalf of commerce or conquest.

●   ●   ●

Being touched by someone with heart is almost unavoidable. Stephen Akhwari and Booker T. Washington captured heart with examples involving competition and an overriding cause. The workplace offers many examples, albeit a bit subtler than these instances. We begin our examination of heart by focusing on one's willingness to work. Often, a remarkable work ethic is not just a tool from which one achieves great success. It is also an indicator of heart.

As the head of the credit card group, Kenneth I. Chenault worked tirelessly to contemporize the brand identity of American Express, pushing the company to enter into markets that had previously been seen as either unworthy or undesirable. His successful efforts played a major role in pulling the company out of a downturn. It was no surprise then that when Chenault was named chairman and CEO of American Express in 2001, many cited his work ethic as the leading reason for his promotion.

Growing up in the card and travel division, Travel Related Services (TRS), Chenault was always intimately aware of the challenges facing the company. The bankcards MasterCard and Visa posed an enormous competitive threat by virtue of their distribution system (the banks), their low-fee proposition, and the choices they offered consumers. Unfortunately, senior management, despite Chenault's efforts, could not be convinced of that threat. "It was hard even to engage people in a discussion of who our competitors were," Chenault later recalled. "The attitude was: 'we really don't have a competitor. We are unique.'"[6]

Change did not begin until March 1992, when the division was informed that American Express would go bankrupt if it did not reduce its operating costs by $1 billion over the next three years. As the senior card executive, Chenault bore the enormous responsibility of finding and implementing the cuts. He succeeded, streamlining the group's operations by reducing the four major credit card lines to a single, minimally staffed unit.

Adjustments continued in 1993, when Chenault was appointed head of the TRS division. Under his leadership, the card group became more dexterous. Merchants, markets, and customers were sought that would expand the brand's identity beyond the traditional high-end entertainment and travel players. The number of new merchant accounts doubled in 1993 to 60,000; the number of card products issued by American Express grew from four to sixty.[7] In the end, Chenault broadened the acceptance and use of American Express products without diluting the value of the American Express brand. Promoted to vice chairman of American Express in 1995, he took the restructuring process that was in place at TRS and applied it to the rest of the company. All told, he was able to eliminate not $1 billion but $3 billion in costs.[8]

Hard work enabled Chenault to change how American Express did business. Harvey Golub, his former supervisor, recalling the crisis year 1992, says of Chenault, "A lot of us were working very hard, but Ken was working the hardest."[9]

Some can say that it was Chenault's desire to get ahead that was the reason for this unmatched work ethic. Doing so, however, would fail to recognize why Chenault was and is such an effective leader. Chenault's work ethic was not born from the need for self-advancement. It came from his passion to implement change and to make improvements.

Working hard to invoke change is an outstanding example of heart. And because of that, its impact can often be felt on more than one level. Chenault worked hard because he felt it immensely important that American Express change the way it operated. By rolling up his sleeves, he became a stronger leader, doing what he was asking others to do, and succeeding in connecting with other people. The end result was the realization of a goal.

Chenault's hard work also paid dividends to people who had little or no relationship with American Express. An African-American, Chenault is not blind to the value he creates by succeeding. While he refuses to make his race the focus of any conversation, by succeeding within the system, he lays the path upon which other African-Americans can walk. By working quietly yet forcefully, he is able to break new ground.[10] Chenault's heart makes him a leader to people other than his coworkers.

●　　●　　●

You cannot teach heart. The best you can do is put people in situations in which they have opportunities to display it. But such passion either exists inside of them or it doesn't. It's not an academic subject; it's an emotional one. Heart isn't a prerequisite for leadership; not every business leader displays this trait, but those who do often capture our attention. If heart is a trait used by a leader, it is not enough that it be translated into an admirable work ethic—endless hours of work can prove monotonous and disheartening. A leader's ability to create positive energy wherever he or she goes is also a clear sign of the trait.

Despite the long hours he spends behind the desk, Kenneth Chenault remains a warm, caring individual who always encourages others: "He's the most human of all chief executives I've worked with," says one associate. "[You] can spend fifteen minutes with Ken and be motivated for the next month without any more contact."[11]

By creating a positive energy, Chenault does not just make the task more bearable; he changes one's perception of what they are doing. It becomes more than work; it becomes something that is invigorating and personally rewarding.

To better explain the ability of some leaders to inspire those around them, we turn to Sam Walton, the founder of Wal-Mart. Walton's ability to create positive energy was fundamental to his company's growth. Without this particular expression of heart, who can say what Wal-Mart would have become?

Like Chenault, Walton had an unbelievable work ethic. Even after he was diagnosed with terminal cancer, he often arrived at the office at 4:30 a.m. and on Saturdays was known to wake up at 3:00 a.m. to review the weekly sales printouts. Early in his career, during family vacations, he insisted on stopping at the local discount stores, curious to see what it was they were doing and whether Wal-Mart could copy them.

However, it was not his work ethic that attracted people. People responded to Sam Walton because of the way he made them feel. The positive energy he brought to Wal-Mart made the company's associates believe they were embarking on an endless adventure instead of just going to work. He did this in a myriad of ways, none more important than another and each equally effective.

First, Walton was practical. To make the associates feel more positive toward the company, he made sure that each of them received a part of the profits. Through programs such as profit sharing, incentive bonuses, and stock purchase plans, the people who handled the goods and faced the customers had a vested interest in doing it the Wal-Mart way.

Second, Walton was generous with praise. Offering comments akin to those of a proud parent rather than an employer, Walton empowered people. Evidence of this generosity of spirit is a visit he made to a store in Memphis, Tennessee, in 1991. Walton talked to as many associates as he possibly could, finding out what they did and how their business was going. But mostly he was there to offer them support and praise:

[Speaking of the new lubrication centers designed to compete with quick oil-change franchises like Jiffy Lube, Walton asks,] "Are these things going to work, Bill?"

"Yes sir, Mr. Sam. They're going to be great."

"Good, good," says Sam.

Moving along toward the pharmacy, [Walton] says, "Hello, Georgie. I like this Equate Baby Oil here for $1.54. I think that's a real winner."

"That's my VPI [volume-producing item]," says Georgie.

Sam whips out his primary tool of empowerment, his tape recorder. "I'm here in Memphis at store 950, and Georgie has done a real fine thing with this endcap display of Equate Baby Oil. I'd like to try this everywhere." Georgie blushes with pride.

A manager rushes up with an associate in tow. "Mr. Walton, I want you to meet Renee. She runs one of the top 10 pet departments in the country."

"Well, Renee, bless your heart. What percentage of the store [sales] are you doing?"

"Last year it was 3.1%," Renee says, "but this year I'm trying for 3.3%.

"Well, Renee, that's amazing," says Sam. "You know our average pet department only does about 2.4%. Keep up the great work."

Sam strolls over to a cashier's stand and picks up a speakerphone—the kind normally reserved for "I need a price check in hardware" and with no introduction calls everyone to the front of the store.

"Northeast Memphis, you're the largest store in Memphis, and you must have the best floor-cleaning crew in America. This floor is so clean—let's sit down on it. [Everyone sits, and Sam crouches on one knee, like a coach designing a play in overtime.] I thank you. The company is so proud of you, we can't hardly stand it. On top of everything else, you went through the trauma of remodeling and still came through with 0.8% shrinkage. [Because the shrinkage, or unaccounted-for loss of inventory, is so low, everyone in the store has recently received a bonus check of several hundred dollars.] Could you use those checks? Were they helpful? Good.

"But you know, that confounded Kmart is getting better, and so is Target. So what's our challenge? Customer service, that's right. Are you thinking about doing those extra little things? Are you lookin' the customer in the eye and offering to help? You know, you're the real reason for Wal-Mart's success. If you don't care about your store and your customers, it won't work. They like the quality and they like the attitude here. They like that we save 'em money, don't they? And they say, 'Hey, something's different about Wal-Mart.'"[12]

Who among us would not want to follow a man so capable of making so many people feel so good about themselves?

Finally, what made Walton so successful at creating positive energy was his ability to make a person's work experience at Wal-Mart fun. This sense of play never compromised the gravity with which he approached the company, but it did much to endear Walton and Wal-Mart to the company's employees. Walton made the mandatory Saturday-morning manager meetings fun. He would often surprise the attendees with special guests like Jack Welch, when he was General Electric's chief executive, or singer Garth Brooks. By offering an alternative to what had been traditionally viewed as mundane, Walton was able to keep his managers interested while getting work done. "Loosen up, and everybody around you will loosen up,"[13] Walton often said, knowing that if he showed enthusiasm about the company and what people did, then soon everyone else would too. The result would be a workforce that was happy to come to work.

It is hard to overlook the passion that Sam Walton brought to his job. Loving what you do is very important, and it is often at the top of the list of reasons why many leaders think they are successful. Yet a person's love for what they do is not a key factor in his or her ability to lead others effectively. By itself, it makes the day enjoyable, but it is not what makes others want to follow or share in a vision.

> If a person would move the world, he must first move himself.
>
> —Socrates[14]

Walton extended his passion to others, making it exciting for them to come to work every day and put forth the effort needed to make Wal-Mart stronger. By sharing his passion and incorporating others into his definition of success, the employees of Wal-Mart were willing to follow him. From that passion comes a positive energy that envelops everyone, particularly to the extent that they too want to make a difference.

Loving your job and creating positive energy are especially helpful to a leader trying to pull a company out of downturn. As chairman and CEO of the McDonald's Corporation, Jim Cantalupo is responsible for serving 46 million customers daily—a number so large it is difficult to fathom. Adding to the challenges inherent in helping so many people is the fact that, when he accepted the job, McDonald's was widely perceived as being in trouble.

Analysts were left disappointed by the company's choice of a thirty-year veteran to rescue it; they had hoped that McDonald's would go outside the company, selecting someone both unbiased and capable of making the changes necessary for the company's return to health. A clear sign of analysts' negative opinion of Cantalupo's appointment was the fact that the company's stock fell 5 percent the day he first spoke with them.

But Cantalupo changed the analysts' minds in a matter of months. TheStreet.com's James J. Cramer originally wrote:

McDonald's still doesn't get it . . . This "change" is just the same old evolution; nothing revolutionary here. In fact, the company is still in massive denial about what is happening. It doesn't recognize that there is a crisis . . . The orchard is rotten.

Yet Cramer was later forced to eat crow, admitting:

I thought I would never write this but the turn is palpable. The company has really gotten its act together. . . . Who knows, maybe you really can change these big companies with change at the top. That's certainly what happened here.[15]

Thus, for there to be change at McDonald's, it was not necessary that the new chairman and CEO come from outside the company. What was necessary, and what proved to be pivotal, was Cantalupo's heart, the passion he had for his new job and his willingness and desire to share that passion with everyone he met.

In his own words: Jim Cantalupo

CANTALUPO SOUNDS LIKE a kid when he talks about his job. His voice is filled with enthusiasm and fervor. It's not what you would expect from a man who retired and then was lured back to take over the helm of the same company he had worked at for thirty years.

"Success in any business is driven by passion. You have to like the business. I can think back to when I was thirteen and started working in a grocery store. I used to love to work on Saturday because of the business that day. It was great to open those doors. That's kind of what McDonald's is like. The lunch rush is exciting. I like the environment and I love the business. To me, that gives you instincts about doing the right thing."

Cantalupo tries hard to share that love for the business with others, wanting them to feel the same energy that brings him to the office every morning. Talking to people, he conveys so much enthusiasm that he never really leaves the room. People are left holding on to his energy, which feeds their own desire to get the job done. The results, of course, are now evident. The job has been getting done, and McDonald's has been able to rebound.

Cantalupo spent most of his career at McDonald's building the international business. "It was a very exhilarating experience. I always said I had the best job in corporate America. It was so exciting to bring McDonald's—a great brand—to all those countries. In the U.S. organization, a lot of things were taken for granted. However, when you had to get potatoes in China or Poland, and it takes seven years to get there, you learn a lot about the basics, but you're also spending a lot of time talking to people, making sure that they always see the value in what they are doing and not getting discouraged."

Cantalupo loved the entrepreneurial world of McDonald's international business. "We grew rapidly. In the U.S., we had a more stable, mature business. [Internationally,] we didn't have that luxury. We would take very young people, ambitious people and get them really excited. They would be twenty-one years old running that first store and three years later they'd be managing director running twenty-five stores, and four years after that at twenty-eight they'd be running the whole country."

Cantalupo took the international business from 2,000 restaurants in 40 countries to 13,000 restaurants in 120. In such a fast-moving environment, picking the right people was critical. "We wanted local talent to run things in their countries. To me, it was spending time with them, getting comfortable and sharing with them what it was we were trying to do and how we wanted to do it. It wasn't asking HR for the 'people who met this list of twenty-three characteristics.' Those people wouldn't have the sense necessary to build the company. The people who got ahead were the people I knew and had spoken to. It was intense."

What Cantalupo has been doing in his new role is nothing different, he thinks, than what he always did overseas. And that is to always bring people back to the basics. Because McDonald's, at its most basic level, is what people can get excited about. Cantalupo believes that McDonald's, for one reason or another, moved away from the basics, resulting in a rather harmful disconnect.

"I spent the last fifteen years around the world eating our food and experiencing our service, using the system that Ray Kroc and Fred Turner developed. In the U.S., we went through several changes [from that original system], which involved our policy about grading restaurants and the way we cooked food. I could taste the difference. I could see that coming from overseas. But when you are living it over a period of ten years in this country, you tend not to notice the shift.

"When I retired and visited a lot of restaurants as a customer, I got a very good education on what the issues [facing the company] were."

In other words, Cantalupo's idea of retiring was to visit McDonald's. He was lured back to a place that many perceived to be going through a tough time. It quickly became apparent to him that analysts were highly skeptical of his approach.

"I accepted that it was a 'show me' environment, so I could either spend my lifetime trying to convince others, or I could go about my business and we could just do it. And that's what we basically did. And the people who were

70

already here got excited. We built that excitement like we did overseas by focusing on the basics, and the system today is on the path back to being known for operational excellence and leadership marketing, the two strengths that we had lost."

Coming out of retirement, Cantalupo is a force of nature, pushing the firm to change. "My theme to the troops is 'We don't want to look like an old chain to our customers.' I remember Howard Johnson's with their blue roofs; they're still around, but where are they? They didn't change enough. In the retail business, you have to stay relevant and current."

Discussing McDonald's new marketing campaign, he points out something that others might easily miss. "The campaign is not just about marketing. It's about motivating a million and a half people." When you have that many employees, you have to think broadly about what it takes to ignite the passion of the team.

"It isn't about getting people to do something," summarizes Cantalupo. "It's about being relevant to their lives."

There are many reasons why Jim Cantalupo has been successful at McDonald's. But the importance of his heart cannot be underestimated. By sharing his passion for the business and the company with others, he created the type of positive environment necessary to bring McDonald's back to health. He fed other people's willingness and desire to do something of value. In turn, they followed him and accomplished just that.

●　　●　　●

In this day and age, when business leaders display heart, we often think of them and their companies as caring for the world around them. They are recognizing goals beyond the bottom line. Some do this on a very personal level, by being altruistic and compassionate, while others lift their concern for society to a much broader stage—defining their companies by it.

The "triple bottom line" is a framework for measuring the performance of corporations not only on an economic level, but also on societal and environmental levels. It's tied to the notion of "sustainability." Novo Nordisk, a healthcare company that is the world's largest producer of insulin, is focused on integrating the triple bottom line in the way it does business. Lars Rebien Sørensen, the firm's president and CEO, wrote, "In our vision of sustainability, corporate commitment is aligned with personal values. To meet the world's immense social and environmental challenges, each of us needs to step on to the scene. More than doing good, we want to do well."[16]

Lise Kingo is an executive vice president at the firm and is both the first woman to be appointed to Novo Nordisk's Executive Committee and the first member of the committee to be dedicated to sustainability. She recently gave an example of the different initiatives the firm is pursuing around the globe:

> One of the initiatives is the World Partner program. We have been analyzing what might constitute a sustainable business model in six different developing countries. In countries where we know that the money available for diabetes patients is very, very limited. How do you make money in a country where people cannot pay for the insulin?
>
> We are in the process of developing a business model where you look much more broadly at the concept of creating business. It's not only about generating good revenue, it's also about creating partnerships with the local patient organizations, and getting in contact with the national health authorities to help them set up a diabetes program, so that diabetes will get on the country's health agenda at all. And it's also about ensuring that we have a new pricing policy where we guarantee that in the less developed countries, the price of insulin will never exceed more than 20 percent of the costs in the developed world.[17]

In 2003, United Parcel Service, Inc. (UPS), released its first corporate sustainability report. In his letter within the report, Mike Eskew, UPS chairman and CEO, explained that he believed the firm's prosperity and sustainability over the coming years was largely dependent on four factors:

> The first is our ability to transform our company to meet the needs of customers and tap into emerging business opportunities.
> The second is our unique and sound business model that maximizes efficiency and generates superior customer benefits with minimal environmental impact—a model that is not easily replicated.
> The third is a culture that promotes human achievement, innovation and results—a philosophy of "constructive dissatisfaction" that is ingrained in all of us. We will not count on our past results to guarantee our future success.
> The fourth is our long-term commitment to the environment and the communities we serve—commitments that stem from the fact that we operate in tens of thousands of communities in more than 200 countries.[18]

Eskew is building on principles put forth by James E. Casey, the man who founded UPS in 1907. He urged employees to practice "constructive dissatisfaction"; never to be fully satisfied and always to look for ways to improve. "Once you make up your mind that you are pretty good," said Casey, "you will no longer feel the urge to do any better." Casey was also fond of saying, "The success of the company has been because we were not working for money alone."[19] Thus UPS, at its very origin, knew the importance of sustainability, of being a good corporate citizen and of showing heart.

Another company that believes that attending to society drives a company's growth is Hewlett-Packard. Carly Fiorina, the company's CEO, has long held that Hewlett-Packard's future growth lies in establishing a presence in the developing world, despite the fact that the vast majority of people living there cannot afford even the most inexpensive of the company's products. Fiorina is so committed to this program, which she has dubbed World e-inclusion, that she created an entire business unit tasked to develop and manage the venture.

What the venture has entailed so far is the following: Hewlett-Packard and its partners have sold, leased or donated more than $1 billion in products and services to governments, development agencies and nonprofit groups in third world countries. The company's early focus has been on systems that help increase the efficiencies of farming, since the livelihoods of more than half the people living in the developing world are derived from the land.

In addition to the introduction of systems and process devices, Hewlett-Packard's World e-inclusion group has worked hard to find and build better methods of financing small entrepreneurs. Working with longtime experts in micro credit, like Bangladesh's Grameen Bank, Hewlett-Packard hopes to build networked devices that will make the lending of credit easier and more efficient.[20]

While the project was founded on the donation of products and services, Hewlett-Packard executives insist that World e-inclusion is not a new word for philanthropy and believe it will offer new ways for the company to generate revenue. They have pointed out on more than one occasion that the systems offered will provide enough value that villagers will purchase them—becoming more informed of the best times and prices to buy and sell their goods. In addition, Hewlett-Packard will profit from the Net-based programs being created to enable individual investors to grant and monitor micro-loans of their own; the company will take a percentage of each loan made.[21]

To Fiorina, e-inclusion is an example of "doing well by doing good." While Hewlett-Packard's brand identity is enhanced as a result of this program, living standards are improved in a number of countries. Fiorina often worries about what might happen if companies like hers did not take such an active role. "Systems in disequilibrium will find equilibrium over time," she says. "If we don't help the system come to a different economic equilibrium, things will begin to happen that we don't care for." [22]

Business leaders with heart are more likely to actively embrace holistic approaches to achieving their vision, approaches like sustainability and social responsibility. These are not in lieu of profitability. Quite the contrary, the goodwill gained from the triple bottom line approach creates a valuable corporate reputation that will make a company less likely to fall victim to bad press or frivolous lawsuits. Viewed as less risky, companies with a triple bottom line have an easier time attracting and retaining stakeholders, including investors, employees, customers and strategic partners. They also have an advantage in securing operating licenses in foreign territories—a company that is known for its exemplary human rights policies and practices will have an easier time obtaining operating licenses in additional markets. Finally, as mentioned in the Hewlett-Packard example, companies that have a demonstrated desire to be socially responsible have increased brand value.

●   ●   ●

Central to the mission of Ben & Jerry's is the belief that all three parts must thrive equally in a manner that commands deep respect for individuals in and outside the company and supports the communities of which they are a part.

Altruism and compassion are elements of heart that come to mind for many as ways of "looking beyond the bottom line." The degree to which leaders can associate the business's objectives with human and societal benefits influences how many constituencies relate to one company versus its competition. Taking care of the environment humanizes a company and active involvement in causes or organizations that help the neediest resonates with employees, shareholders and host communities alike.

> Ben & Jerry's is founded on and dedicated to a sustainable corporate concept of linked prosperity. The company's mission consists of three interrelated parts; all of which have to thrive equally in a manner that *commands deep respect for individuals in and outside the company and support the communities in which they are a part.*[23]
>
> **Product Mission**
> To make, distribute and sell the finest quality all natural ice cream & euphoric concoctions with a continued commitment to incorporating wholesome, natural ingredients and promoting business practices that respect the Earth and the Environment.
>
> **Economic Mission**
> To operate the Company on a sustainable financial basis of profitable growth, increasing value for our stakeholders and expanding opportunities for development and career growth for our employees.
>
> **Social Mission**
> To operate the company in a way that actively recognizes the central role that business plays in society by initiating innovative ways to improve the quality of life locally, nationally and internationally

Arthur Blank, owner of the Atlanta Falcons football team, makes sure that his players realize their value to the Atlanta community. He told us, "When I first bought the team, I told everyone that from my viewpoint there are two Super Bowls every year. One is played on the field, but the other one is played off the field in the community. It's about being a leader in our community. I want our players and our coaches and the whole organization to represent themselves well and be Falcons' ambassadors in the city, in the region and in the state—to have a real sense of giving back to the community.

"It's all part of creating an organization people are very proud to be a part of. Because at the end of the day, players are players, and coaches are coaches, but they also want to feel like they are part of an organization that means something more than just going out and playing for sixty minutes on Sunday. When they tell their neighbors they play for the Atlanta Falcons, they want their neighbors to think highly of them not just because the team is a good, but because the team represents a group of people who are very good citizens."

As an example of what Blank is talking about, in 2002 the Falcons community relations department introduced the Ball Boy Mentoring Program, which was designed to keep the players involved in the lives of the boys who help the equipment staff during training camp and throughout the season. The players serve as counselors to these young men through monthly meetings that provide the boys the opportunity to speak to the players about the things that may be impacting their lives.[24]

Businesses that look beyond financial returns and display a commitment to giving back to the community enjoy a connection with people that enhances the good times and offers resilience during the bad times. Being a good corporate citizen, however, is rarely as cut and dry as one might think.

Yvon Chouinard, founder of outdoor clothing manufacturer Pantagonia, Inc., lives by rules that connect him in a deep way with the people and the world around him. For example, long ago he started drinking from every stream in which he fishes. Why? He decided, "I'd be outside the rest of my life, so I had to adapt. I've gotten sick a lot, but each time I got stronger and less sick."[25]

NBC News anchor Tom Brokaw, one of Chouinard's climbing companions, told the *New York Times*, "Yvon's idea of comfort is spending the night halfway up a mountain sharing half a submarine sandwich while wrapped in a nylon shroud when a cold front comes in."

Brokaw added, "We call ourselves the do-boys," he added. "We go do things."[26]

Chouinard's passion and determined approach to life set the tone for the company he founded and the brand he built. He is the type of man who inspires employees as well as customers. But he is not an unbridled risk taker, nor does he let his passionate nature overwhelm his better judgment.

When Chouinard takes on new challenges, he never loses sight of his limits. Using a climbing analogy, he states, "If you're a 5.10 climber [referring to level of difficulty], you sure as hell don't go solo a 5.11. You live within your means."[27] Chouinard takes this same attitude when running his company. Success, to him, is always dependent on one's understanding of the risks. If the risks are too great, no matter one's passion, the better course is always to find alternatives.

For heart to be a truly effective trait, it cannot stand alone. There must exist some type of thought process so that there is balance when making a decision. This calming influence can come from anywhere, but what is most important is that it is always present. The relationship between passion and prudence is often what separates effective leaders from wild-eyed fanatics. It provides much-needed control, mitigating the potential risk of decisions made from the heart.

Over the years, Patagonia has tried hard to be a good corporate citizen. One of the "greenest" businesses around, it was the first apparel maker to use recycled soda bottles to make synthetic fleece sweaters and warm-up pants. It was also one of the first companies to use organic cotton to make clothes— eating half of the 20 percent markup that organic materials added to the production cost. Its glossy catalog, printed on recycled paper that is 50 percent chlorine-free, uses pictures of adventurers in wild places to promote environmental causes.[28]

Few have ever questioned the company's motivations or Chouinard's heart. Recently, however, realities have encroached upon the company, and the extent to which heart can build and sustain a successful business has been brought into question. In a recent letter to customers, the company admonished itself for depending on bright dyes, which come from strip-mined metals, and Gore-Tex, which contains chemical toxins. Only through these products, the company admits, is it able to produce the clothes people have come to love. Thus, despite its best efforts, Patagonia's production of clothing is having a negative impact the earth.

In this situation, if Chouinard were to remain true to his heart, which is to run a company that is environmentally friendly, then he would insist that Patagonia move away from Gore-Tex and bright dyes. Doing so, however, would diminish the quality of Patagonia's products. Water-based coatings, which are both safer and more environmentally friendly to manufacture than Gore-Tex, are not durable enough to stay waterproof. Only 20 percent of the company's customers buy from Patagonia because they support its environmental mission, thus a move away from Gore-Tex and bright dyes would result in the company taking a large financial hit—from which it might not recover.

Sometimes the risk related to the displaying of heart is so great that alternatives need to be found. Chouinard is not blind to this. He knows that if Patagonia is to continue to thrive as a business, it cannot be run with a focus only on the goals that exist beyond the bottom line. Financial considerations must weigh in and consensus is essential. Thus, for the survival of the business, it has to be enough that Patagonia represents "the best quality at the lowest environmental impact" instead of "the best quality at no environmental impact."

●   ●   ●

When we talk of things like corporate social responsibility and a company's success at meeting the triple bottom line, we are still speaking in the terms of business and performance. In these examples, companies are doing good, and it is hard sometimes for people to relate directly to companies. The concept of business, especially at the highest levels, is opaque to many and lacks immediacy. Much easier is it for people to relate to other people. This is why showing compassion is such an effective way for a business leader to connect with others.

People like working for a company that has shown itself to be a good corporate citizen, but how much more connected are they, and how much more willing are they to follow direction, when they have firsthand experience of seeing an executive display empathy?

In 2002, Microsoft founder and chairman Bill Gates and his wife, Melinda, gave away more than $1 billion through the Bill and Melinda Gates Foundation. The foundation has ambitious goals, such as the reduction of the "unconscionable disparity that exists between the way that we live and that people of the developing world live." It is also tackling difficult challenges such as AIDS, poverty, education, and the digital divide.

Gates says that next to playing with his kids and spending time with his family, one of the most satisfying parts of his life is "the impact that [the foundation has] on a worldwide basis, the excitement of taking the latest medical technology and saying, 'Okay, there's this poor guy who's been wanting to work on malaria his whole life and nobody pays attention, nobody gives him money.' And then we can come along and say 'Hey, you are doing God's work. This is so important. Here, we'll fund your malaria vaccine.'" [29]

As he was on his way to becoming the richest man in the world, Gates was often criticized for not giving back. He listened to that criticism and now applies as much heart to his selected causes as he did to building one of the most successful companies of the twentieth century. The result, we think, is a leader who is easier to relate to and one more likely to be embraced by his subordinates.

John W. Rogers Jr. shares Gates's satisfaction with giving back to the community. In fact, he told us that he thinks of the two as being interwoven. Rogers is chairman, CEO and chief investment officer of Ariel Capital Management, a firm he founded in 1983, when he was just twenty-four years old.

In his own words: John W. Rogers Jr.

"WHEN I CAME back to Chicago," Rogers explains, "I felt like I was part of the 'Chicago team.' There is a real connection in this town between community service and business leadership. It works well together, and everyone encourages you, and pushes you to do it. Community service is so important to all the business leaders here."

Early on, Rogers joined the Urban League board, where he got the chance to work with leaders running major businesses who were also giving time to the community. As the youngest member of the board, he was "highly impressionable" and started looking for opportunities to help. He found the ideal platform upon which to assist the community when he teamed with childhood friend Arne Duncan, and Duncan's sister, Sarah, to create the Ariel Foundation.

Rogers explains the foundation's accomplishments: "It created the 'I Have a Dream' program in Chicago, where a group of sixth-grade students were adopted and given the promise that college would be made affordable for them. The foundation also created the Ariel Community Academy, which is a small public school that the firm has sponsored for the past seven years." The school now has over 350 students and represents a unique partnership with the city of Chicago.

"It was Arne and Sarah's vision," admits Rogers. "I may have chimed in from time to time, but they created it. I've known [Arne] since the fifth grade. Pretty much every day after school, he went to where his mother was tutoring inner-city schoolchildren. When we created this program with Ariel, we thought, who better to turn to than Arne?"

Rogers chose well. In 2001, at age thirty-seven, Arne Duncan became CEO of the Chicago Public Schools. He still serves on the board of the Ariel Education Initiative.

Despite Rogers' modesty, the more he talks, the more it becomes clear how involved he has been. "Primarily, what [we are] in charge of is the after-school programming to make the school day extended, so kids have a place to go to keep learning and to be nurtured. We put in place a full-time curriculum director. We also created a savings and investment program for the kids, where every first-grade class gets a $20,000 class gift from Ariel and other partners. The kids watch the money grow until sixth grade, when they start to pick stocks. A full-time teacher works with the kids, helping them execute their savings and investment plans."

Rogers embodies what we mean by heart. He had the passion and drive to launch his own business at age twenty-four. In doing so, he became one of the first African-Americans to run an investment company. He had the staying power to keep pushing for several years, until he won his first client, the Municipal Employees' Annuity & Benefit Fund of Chicago. And along the way, he has not only made sure that his company has looked way beyond the bottom line, but he has also never surrendered his compassion.

• • •

In partnership with Daniel Yankelovich, Russell Reynolds Associates examined what it would take for business leaders to regain the trust lost as a result of the financial scandals that have hit some of the world's most widely known companies over the past few years. The conclusion was that much of the public's faith would be restored if companies and business leaders adhered to strategies that in, some way, displayed heart. Or, more matter of factly, people's trust in companies would increase if specific values were recognized, including, but not limited to:

- Respect for customers, employees, host communities, and stakeholders
- Commitment to exemplary corporate behavior
- Sustained economic performance with a view for the long term
- Humanization of the corporate entity to its stakeholders[30]

Again, the formula is practical. "The business of business is business" is the attitude that governed for some time. In today's world, the need to be profitable, provide jobs, and create products and services needed by society are what business does best. Yet, due to the stresses on our environment and severe gaps between the "haves" and "have nots," business today is expected to go beyond simply being a good investment for shareholders and a contributor to economies.

Perhaps because business has more flexibility than many government organizations to attack specific problems, business is in a unique position to help address society and environment issues that impact all of our lives. Finding the right niche to do so, committing to that niche and delivering on a promise "to do something" is a realistic expectation of business leaders. We believe those who do this will stand out among their peers as the true leaders in the years to come.

As a leader, you need to ask yourself what important issue your organization can do something about and find the resolve to take on the challenge. No one can change the world; a single leader or company cannot fully solve any of the major issues society and the environment face. However, each company has something to contribute to the solution of a given challenge. Finding a challenge your company is best suited for and then championing that cause is worthy of you as a leader.

For those who are seeking leaders for their companies, looking beyond the CV and into a candidate's heart may be a bit unconventional, but failing to do so will prevent you from finding the leaders that can take your organization to its ultimate potential. Fortunately, those who have heart usually display the trait quite naturally, through their previous work experiences, their involvement in community and family and through passionate expression of what really motivates them.

A perspective from the Russell Reynolds Associates Executive Assessment Team

In order for humanitarian efforts to be accepted by the organization and the public, the leaders of the organization must demonstrate true commitment to the efforts. Although environmental or humanitarian sensitivity may often appeal to consumers, it is important that the efforts be perceived as an honest commitment and not just a marketing ploy.

Such commitment must be ingrained into the culture of the company. This can be achieved in several ways. First, the leaders of the organization must effectively communicate a sincere interest and commitment to the cause. By continually bringing such issues to the attention of employees in written and oral communications, members of the organization will come to accept the issue as a priority. Second, participating in programs around these efforts makes the sincerity of the effort highly visible. In addition, supporting individuals who contribute to the efforts financially and with time conveys the importance of realizing such goals.

Many CEOs perceive connecting their organization to the community as an integral part of their job. The benefits of contributing to the community can be very rewarding for individuals within the company and often also serve the business in a positive way. For example, participation in charitable events provides excellent networking opportunities for employees to meet individuals in similar businesses and to meet with potential clients. In addition, associating with charitable organizations provides a positive connotation for the company that is often attractive to potential clients or customers.

Wal-Mart, for example, has received positive press for being prominent in supporting community programs. Encouraging employees to become involved in charitable groups often allows them to socialize with coworkers in a positive way, improving working relationships and increasing their commitment and sense of

sources

1. *The Forbes Book of Business Quotations*, ed. Ted Goodman (New York: Black Dog & Leventhal Publishers, 1997), p. 399.

2 .Selected quote, "Heart," Mark Twain letter to Alvert Sonnichsen, 1901, www.twainquotes.com (accessed February 13, 2004).

3. Stephen Akhwari's response to Bud Greenspan's question, 1968 Olympics, Mexico City, http://espn.go.com/page2/s/questions/budgreenspan.html (accessed February 1, 2004).

4. Emmett J. Scott (Emmett Jay), and Lyman Beecher Stowe, *Booker T. Washington: Builder of a Civilization* (New York: Doubleday, Page & Company, 1916), p. xi. Full text available at http://docsouth.unc.edu/neh/scott/menu.html(accessed February 22, 2004).

5. Booker T. Washington, *Up from Slavery: An Autobiography* (New York: Doubleday & Co., c. 1901), p. 243. Full text available at http://docsouth.unc.edu/washington/washing.html (accessed February 22, 2004).

6. Anthony Bianco, "The Rise of a Star," *Business Week*, December 21, 1998, p. 60.

7. Ibid.

8. Marjorie Whigham-Desir, "Leadership Has Its Rewards: Ken Chenault's Low-key yet Competitive Style Has Pushed Him up the Executive Ladder and to the CEO's Chair," *Black Enterprise*, Septemper 30, 1999, p. 73.

9. Anthony Bianco, "The Other Side of Ken Chenault," *Business Week*, December 21, 1998, p. 65.

10. Ron Stodghill, "Eyes on the Prize at Amex," *Business Week*, September 13, 1993, p. 59.

11. Ponchitta Pierce, "Kenneth Chenault: Blazing New Paths in Corporate America," *Ebony*, July, 1997, p. 58.

12. John Huey, "America's Most Successful Merchant," *Fortune*, September 23, 1991, p. 46.

13. Marilyn Much, "Sam Walton the Energizer," *Investor's Business Daily*, February 9, 1998.

14. Selected quote, "Heart," http://www.humanistsofutah.org/quotes.html (accessed February 22, 2004).

15. Whitney Tilson, "CEO of the Year: McDonald's Cantalupo." *Motley Fool*, October 10, 2003, http://www.fool.com/news/commentary/2003/commentary031017wt.htm (accessed February 22, 2004).

16. *Sustainability Report 2003*, Corporate Communications, http://www.novonordisk.com /sustainability/sustainability_report_2002/ceo_statement.asp(accessed February 22, 2004).

17. Leadership Example," Novo Nordisk: Integrating CSR into Business Operations ," BSR, June 2002, http://www.bsr.org/BSRResources/Magazine/Leadership.cfm?DocumentID=767 (accessed February 22, 2004).

18. Mike Eskew, letter from the chairman, http://www.sustainability.ups.com/letter.htm (accessed February 22, 2004).

19. Patty Mayeux, "Delivering Success," *Y & E: The Magazine for Teen Entrepreneurs*, May 2001, http://ye.entreworld.org/5-2001/jamesecasey.cfm(accessed February 22, 2004).

20. David Kirkpatrick, "Looking for Profits in Poverty," *Fortune*, February 5, 2001, p. 174.

21. Ibid.

22. Ibid.

23. Ben & Jerry's official website, "Mission Statement," http://www.benjerry.com/ourcompany/ our_mission/(accessed February 20, 2004).

24. The official Atlanta Falcons website, "Community Outreach," http://www.atlantafalcons.com/community/001/122/ (accessed March 8, 2004).

25. Monte Burke, "The World According to Yvon" *Forbes*, November 26, 2001.

26. Patricia Leigh Brown, "The Maverick Who Sent America Outdoors," *New York Times*, March 11, 1998.

27. Ibid.

28. Paul C. Judge, "It's Not Easy Being Green," *BusinessWeek*, November 24, 1997, p. 180.

29. H. Darr Beiser, "Gates on What's Worthwhile," *USA Today*, June 30, 2003, http://www.usatoday.com/tech/news/2003-06-29-gates-worthwhile_x.htm (accessed February 22, 2004).

30. *Leadership and Public Trust in Business*, Corporate Communications (New York: Russell Reynolds Associates, 2003).

5

Team Building

The important thing to recognize is that it takes a team, and the team ought to get credit for the wins and the losses. Successes have many fathers, failures have none.

—Philip Caldwell, former chairman, Ford Motor Company; current board member, Russell Reynolds Associates[1]

One hand cannot applaud alone.
—Arabian proverb[2]

THE BEST ORGANIZATIONS are not dependent on any one person; they are self-sustaining entities in which many people and processes work together toward a common purpose.

Those who aspire to build an organization that is bigger than themselves recognize the importance of team building. They invest time, money, and thought in creating a unified and energized team.

In many cases, such leaders also create a culture in which accomplished employees mentor others. Such care and attention sends a message: you are a valued member of the team, and your future is our future.

Beyond that, the sense of community fostered by a team environment satisfies the natural human need to affiliate. Many experts cite the lack of community as one of the greatest ailments afflicting modern society. Providing community contributes to employees' psychic well-being as well as their financial and personal well-being.

No business or organization will succeed if that success rests on the shoulders of just one person. Goals can only be met when people work together. The ability to build a team capable of helping a company realize its ambitions is a trait that has proven to be fundamental to the success of many leaders.

Much goes into the building of an effective team. It is not just the process of bringing people together, providing guidance and then evaluating how they do it. The leader as team builder is attentive to many things beyond the most obvious. It begins with a clear vision with which the team can connect. Team builders devote a great deal of effort to foster pride within the team. The team builder encourages mentorship and places great emphasis on how each individual can do better as a result of being part of the team. Team builders pay attention to the structure of the organization and apply processes that both encourage and reward the success of team behavior. They create an environment in which team members' trust of one another minimizes uncertainty, and individuals' weaknesses are diminished by the strengths of others. When all of these elements come together, the results are monumental and much greater than what any one individual alone could accomplish or direct.

●　　●　　●

There are all kinds of teams. We tend to think of teams as many people working together, but most effective organizations have an array of teams, sometimes consisting of just two or three people.

The early success of Deutsche Bank can be attributed to a number of things, yet few are as important as the management team put together by bank founder and supervisory board chair Adelbert Delbrück. Delbrück sought a strategy from the board of managing directors that would enable the bank to become a global power in trade finance, a market then dominated by large British institutuions. He selected Georg Siemens to be spokesman, the managing board's leader among equals, but made sure he worked closely with director Hermann Wallich, who knew far more about banking and international finance than did Siemens. The talents and experiences of the two men were such that each man's strengths perfectly complemented the other's, resulting in a team that successfully drove Deutsche Bank's early gains in international trade finance.

Recalling the nature of their relationship, Wallich said:

Frequently Siemens and I disagreed over one or other of the audacious proposals he came up with. More often than not, however, sometimes even against my better judgment, I let him have his way, an unconscious instinct telling me: "You can't allow this fellow to go. He is an enormous asset to the bank and possesses qualities that you yourself lack." In moments of crisis, on the other hand, my expereince and conservative principles prevailed. Siemens called me the bank's conscience. Anyhow, a large firm like ours had room for more than one man of talent. In good times, possibly my younger colleague's fire was more useful than my own perhaps over-cautious, if not downright old-fashioned, style of management.[3]

Though lost somewhat in the shadow of Wallich, and certainly in that of Siemens, Delbrück was a man who understood that great things can happen if people of different skill sets are given a forum in which they can work together and trust one another. Simply having and acting on this understanding made him an effective leader. By teaming Siemens with Wallich, men with very different talents, Delbrück better guaranteed that Deutsche Bank would become a global power in trade finance.

It is clear that Delbrück was successful in building a team that was "greater" than he was. What these men accomplished working together was far greater than what any one of them could have done working alone. The present stature of Deutsche Bank is evidence of that.

Another, more recent example of how a team can achieve greater deeds than any individual is the comeback story of U.S. motorcycle manufacturer Harley-Davidson.

It began in 1981, when Vaughn Beals led the company's management team in one of the largest leveraged buyouts to that point in history. At the time, Harley-Davidson earned nearly $300 million in annual revenue and with just $1 million in equity, the group was able to finance the roughly $70 million purchase price.

In his own words: Vaughn Beals

BEALS RECALLS, "MY wife and I had put up $220,000 in capital; we had little left. If this had failed, I was going to be close to sixty without any resources and with no pension. We bet everything we had; in hindsight, it was not a rational thing to do. It involved a gross amount of chutzpah.

"Timing had a lot to do with our ability to pull the deal off, though. In 1980, the deal would have been viewed as impossibly large; by 1982, the amount would have been mocked as trivial. The state of the investment banking business was just where we needed it to be."

Aside from the financial hurdles, Harley-Davidson had to overcome other huge challenges if the company were to survive. Low-priced Japanese motorcycles were invading the market. The American manufacturer's quality was comparatively low—but improving—and its prices were high. Furthermore, in late 1985, as the company's market share was growing and after it had enjoyed three consecutive years of positive cash flow, the group's lead lender decided that it wanted to liquidate the firm. Thus, for a few months, Beals and his team faced the new obstacle of bankruptcy. Fortunately, support remained from three other banks, and in December 1985, the company was refinanced. Soon thereafter, Harley-Davidson was listed on the American Stock Exchange, and in June 1987 the company made its first appearance on the New York Stock Exchange.[4]

Ultimately, Beals readily admits, the success of Harley-Davidson was more about the work of the group rather than anything he might have done by himself. Emphasizing this point, he mentions that he did not say anything at group meetings that his managers called—he was there to show support for the group's efforts.

"As a CEO you are grossly outnumbered," says Beals. "I have seen some CEOs—and have fired some managers—who thought they were smarter than all the people who worked for them. Anybody who thinks that—and you can read about it in the newspapers every day—is totally wrong. What got the company from there to here was letting the people who knew what needed to be done do it. Time and again, when asked to describe his leadership style, Beals says that he tried to give each person what he or she needed. "Some people would say it was dictatorial, others would say it was participatory. But some required a dictatorial approach; others required the opposite."

Beals understood that the people who really did the work had valuable knowledge that he needed to tap. That knowledge came not just from working closely with the product, it also came from conversations Harley-Davidson management had with the company's customers. Beals explains,

"The thing that differentiates Harley from its competition was that no motorcycle race or rally took place without Harley management in attendance. That's just the lifestyle of the company. You went and rode motorcycles with the customers.

"If there was a problem with a new product, you found out about it at the rally and addressed it the next day. You didn't have to wait for dealers to report problems and the service department to figure them out.

"If you looked around at the rallies for our competitors' management, what you found was junior staff with cameras and notebooks looking at the Harleys, jotting down notes and photographing details. But you never, ever saw the senior or higher management."

The impetus of Harley-Davidson's turnaround and eventual resurgence underlines how important the intelligence gathered by people and the building of teams was to the company's success. Beals tells us, "We concluded that . . . we'll never be able to beat the Japanese on quality; they set very high standards. It's tough to beat them on costs. So we have to beat them someplace else. In 1982, we had a three-day off-site management meeting, during which we came up with the idea of an owner's group. Three or four months later we established H.O.G., the Harley Owners Group The great thing about H.O.G. is that it keeps the company, both management and employees, in touch with their customers and what they like and dislike about the product."[5]

H.O.G. started slowly but gained momentum, and ultimately became the largest factory-sponsored motorcycle club in the world. Today it has over 750,000 paid members. In a sense, H.O.G. is a team built by Beals to reestablish and perpetuate Harley-Davidson's brand identity. It has been successful in ways that no company employee or advertising campaign could be. By inviting the company's customers to join the Harley-Davidson team, Beals successfully used their product loyalty as the force to drive the company forward.

Recently, Harley-Davidson celebrated its one hundredth anniversary, and the twentieth anniversary of H.O.G.; 120,000 people showed up with their motorcycles. Few companies could attract so many customers to a birthday party. The fact that Harley-Davidson is still around to do so is a testament not just to the power of its working teams but also to the leaders who realized that in order to survive, Harley-Davidson needed many people to work together.

• • •

The idea of the team as greater than any one individual means more than extending the capabilities of a business. Beyond liberating a business from the limitations of any one person, a true team is able to achieve a company's goals in the event of a succession or, more generally, a leader's absence.

A CEO cannot be in all places at all times, and every CEO's term ends at some point. Building an effective team requires the leader to entrust others with responsibility, to allow them to make important decisions. By sharing the challenges facing the organization with the team, a leader instills a greater sense of proprietorship, cohesiveness, and belonging within the group. The result is a more expansive notion of ownership, which is essential if a company is to realize its long-term goals. All participants care about the greater good of the organization and behave accordingly when they have skin in the game, sweat equity, part ownership. And information and participation count every bit as much as financial equity in terms of creating behavior that screams "team."

> The leaders who work most effectively, it seems to me, never say "I." And that's not because they have trained themselves not to say "I." They don't think "I." They think "we"; they think "team." They understand their job to be to make the team function. They accept responsibility and don't sidestep it, but "we" gets the credit . . . This is what creates trust, what enables you to get the task done.
>
> —Peter Drucker[6]

This idea was not lost on Vaughn Beals, nor is it lost now on his successor, Jeff Bleustein, current chairman and CEO of Harley Davidson who stated in a 2001 speech:

> Partnering has fundamentally changed the way we do business. It's made Harley-Davidson a better place to work and, in the process, it's made our business more successful than ever . . .
>
> Leadership is shared. Decisions are made jointly. Employees are empowered. They are empowered to make decisions at their work place, because they are the closest to the work and they know what they need in order to get the job done. But also, they are empowered to make decisions and are involved in decisions about other things, such as strategy, new products, and so forth. We are really trying to encourage

the best that each of our employees has to give. . . .

Financial rewards are shared with all employees. Every person at Harley-Davidson is on an incentive program, and the key thing is, it's the same incentive program for everyone—from the factory floor to the executive office, we're all working by the same formula. So when I have a good payday, so do the people in the factories and the accounting department—we all share in it alike.[7]

Two leaders who were effective in building businesses that encouraged the professional growth of others, assuring that the company's vision would be maintained in their absence, were August Thyssen and Alfred Sloan, Jr. Despite their different objectives and the fact that they worked in different industries, countries, and times, Thyssen and Sloan devised remarkably similar ways in which their employees could be empowered.

The German business environment was in flux during much of Thyssen's tenure as executive officer first of Thyssen & Co. and then of Thyssen-Konzern.[8] Otto von Bismarck, Germany's first chancellor, had only recently unified the various German states when the initial company was founded in 1871. And though the steel manufacturer grew up behind the walls of tariff protection, Thyssen did have to navigate the fluctuations of a strong yet emerging economy. Specifically, he had to face down the challenges posed by the presence of cartels in Germany and the financial strains put upon his companies by World War I. A man in constant search of ways to strengthen his interests, Thyssen relied most heavily on the wherewithal and innovative intelligence of his management teams.

The approach Thyssen took to building teams was in many ways a precursor to the innovative management strategies developed by Sloan when he was president of General Motors. Because of it, Thyssen & Co. was able to weather the challenges of the market, surviving when similar firms faltered or were consolidated, and Thyssen-Konzern was able to realize advantages that other large corporations could not.

Thyssen organized his companies into various product departments, each responsible for both production and sales. The department heads were responsible for almost all of the adminstrative work associated with the running of the group, including the hiring and firing of workers and the determining of wages, defined by a given range. Working with central accounting, each deparment also handled its own inventories and assessed its own capital assets. Departments were seen as near autonomous commercial centers, not just production locales. Consequently, managers, unlike their counterparts elsewhere, were required to think not only of operating methodologies but were also obligated to attend to the needs of commerce. How much they were paid depended on how successful they were in marrying these vastly different skill sets.[9]

By entrusting responsibility to others, Thyssen succesfully built decentralized companies that were better able to react to the market. While he remained the ultimate decision maker, a select group of managers actually ran his operations.

As an illustration of how he delgated responsibilities, Thyssen once sent Julius Kalle, a new director of GDK, a company in which Thyssen had controlling interest and which would later be a part of Thyssen-Konzern, to America to study the latest strip-steel techniques. On the recommendation of the twenty-seven-year-old, Thyssen purchased the license to an American-style cold-rolling strip steel mill. For the next twenty-five years, the mill was the only one of its type in Europe, proving to be highly profitable.[10]

Comparatively, company dynamics rather than market challenges drove Sloan to change the relationship between the senior executive and other employees. General Motors was a organization of many divisions; some were responsible for producing different models of cars and trucks, others were committed only to the manufacturing of parts. To operate efficiently, GM could not allocate the responsibilities of its managers according to their functions, as was done in most U.S. companies. Nor could it adhere to the common practice of having all functional department heads report to a single person. If business suffered, there was nowhere to look but to the chief executive, and there was no way of knowing where the problems had manifested themselves.

A centralized, functionally compartmentalized organizational structure is best used by small companies or large firms that focus on one product type, like coal. What GM needed was something different. Referred to by economists simply as the M-form, Sloan's solution is recognized as one of the great institutional advances in American business history and has proven to be so fundamentally sound that it was able to accommodate the exponential growth of GM, even as the company surpassed 500,000 employees.[11]

What makes the M-form organization unique is that, within it, division heads are given total profit-and-loss responsibility for the products and/or services under their control. Similar in effect to the changes implemented by Thyssen, the M-form was able to combine the benefits gained from central control with those from decentralized decision making. Various levels of authority were introduced to the company, resulting in operational order; because there were more checks and balances the company became more efficient, making it less likely that any one problem would become so overwhelming that it could handicap the entire organization.

Individual value was also maximized within the new system. The working capacity of each employee increased; work was no longer stopped for long periods of time as people waited for solutions to problems or answers to questions. Further, as people proved themselves, they climbed higher within the company and were given more and greater responsibilities. As a result, their roles became increasingly more important to GM's operations and the company was able to get much more out of them.

The M-form was Sloan's successful attempt at building strong teams inside GM. The dynamics of the company were such that the only way it could survive would be as a result of a number of different people sharing the control and leadership functions. Without this dispersion of authority, chaos would reign. Sloan would have been flooded with information, incapacitated to the point of being unable to act. And even if he could act, most likely either it would be too late or he would be misinformed as to the true nature of the problem. The M-form, because it led to more effective teams, provided GM with more points of contact to the market, to customers, to problems. It enabled GM to operate efficiently and to grow.

By empowering others, Thyssen and Sloan benefitted their respective companies. Both GM and Thyssen-Konzern were able to flourish as a result of their innovations, opportunites were increased because trust was placed in others and missteps were avoided. Thyssen and Sloan equipped others with the tools necessary to overcome the challenges facing their respective companies. They better guaranteed that no challenge would be missed, that no obstacle would grow so big as to handicap the business's growth.

One of the many virtues of the M-form was that it provided a way for large numbers of managers to become more involved with how General Motors conducted its business. With the introduction of the new structure, there came a great number of cross-division committees. Working with one another, managers became more aware of the company's challenges and were better able to respond.[12]

Teamwork is about shared ownership. The ability to build a team is fundamental to good leadership, because for a business to be sucessful over the long term, ownership has to be shared. Thyssen and Sloan shared their leadership with others and by doing so their companies were immeasurably improved by the efforts of such men as Donaldson Brown and Charles Kettering at GM, and Franz Dahl and Julius Kalle at Thyssen-Konzern.

William Wrigley Jr., the chairman and CEO of the Wm. Wrigley Jr. Company, is a firm believer in shared ownership. He is able to trust his team with important tasks because he believes shared ownership is about trust, dignity, and respect.

"It's easy for people to say 'trust,' but if you truly give someone your trust, they will want to succeed. I've found that if you have good people who are well trained and have the right resources, then, typically, they're smart enough not to get into a lot of trouble and capable enough to do something that goes beyond expectations. So long as they have some checks and balances that aren't too oppressive, a group of people can really do a lot more than any one person, and the company is much better off."

•   •   •

When we think of shared ownership, an important by-product is the idea that there will be someone capable of taking the business leader's place when the time comes for him or her to retire. We have touched briefly on this already, but it is important for us to emphasize now how vital teams are to the successful succession of executive officers. They allow a number of people to become intimately involved with the operations of the company, enabling them to gain an understanding of how divisions, other then their own, function. Strong teams provide a company with large pools of potential candidates who are capable of replacing any business executive; men and women who are not only familiar enough with the operations of the company to effectively take on greater responsibilities, but who also have proven themselves capable of handling those responsibilities by overcoming challenges.

There is no greater illustration of how effective empowering others is to the fluid succession of executive officers than General Electric. We are all aware of the well-deserved kudos of the company's former CEO Jack Welch. However, Welch did not come to the position as some outside white knight tasked to save a failing company. He was a homegrown talent, the product of a system that had been put in place over a half century before by CEO Charles Coffin, who believed that the company's survival depended on each generation of GE employees being trained to replace the last. The GE that Welch inherited from his predecessor, Reginald Jones, was also in good shape. In financial terms, the company performed as well under Jones's eight-year tenure as CEO as it did during the first eight years of Welch's leadership.[13]

Entrusting others with responsibility and demanding that they prove themselves prior to being given greater responsibility has proved to be a highly effective strategy for General Electric. Each of the company's seminal leaders was a product of it. Welch began his management career at GE as the general manager of the polymer products division in 1964. While his exuberance and impatience led some to think him rude and cavalier, his results could not be questioned. Overcoming the initial failures of a blended plastics design, he and his team produced Noryl, a product that today has more than $1 billion in worldwide sales.[14] By meeting the challenges he faced head on and working with others to come up with solutions, Welch positioned himself to take on more responsibility. Having proven what he was capable of, in 1968 Welch was promoted to general manager of the plastics business. Not long after that, in 1971, he was named vice president of the chemical and metallurgical division.

Welch's rise at GE was a result of the leadership skills of two men, first chairman and CEO Fred Borch and then Jones. Both accepted the corporate mantra that the building of good teams was imperative to their roles as leaders. Teams dealt with the challenges facing the company, allowing it to grow, but they also presented to the senior leadership the people who would be most capable of taking the reins of authority in the future and of maintaining GE's core value system. Because Welch was able to continually show his worth to the company, communicating with and working well with others, it was only a matter of time before he came to be viewed as a potential successor to Jones.

But that is not to say that Welch was the only one. Again, the beauty of numerous strong teams is that they provide multiple strong candidates for leadership positions. For the CEO position, Jones had the good fortune of being able to choose among a number of outstanding performers. Once the field had been whittled down to six, he made each a sector executive, reporting directly to him, so he could better test and observe the candidates' abilities. Thus, by further sharing his leadership role with a new team and opening the company up to it, Jones made sure that GE remained in good standing after his retirement.

Jones made these comments when promoting Welch as one of the six: "I think highly of you, but, Jack, you don't understand General Electric. You've only seen 10 percent of the company. GE's a lot more than that. I have a new job for you—sector executive for the consumer products businesses. But, Jack, this job is in Fairfield. You can't be a big fish in a small pond anymore. If you want to be considered for bigger things, you're going to have to come here." [15]

General Electric's fortunes would only be maintained if Welch and the other sector executives were granted greater access to departments other than their own. By sharing this knowledge, Jones was trying to find out who could work well with others and who was the most capable of making the types of decisions necessary for GE to maintain the leadership position it had held for much of the twentieth century.

When we speak of the example of GE, we are illustrating how important teams are to internal succession. Strong teams are also helpful when a new executive officer comes from the outside. As the new executive becomes familiar with the company, existing teams provide continuity to keep the company strong during the changeover.

●　　●　　●

Implicit in the idea of a team is a group of people united in a common purpose. In most cases, but not all, the team is competing against others. United Airlines competes against American Airlines, American Express competes against Visa, and Coca-Cola competes against Pepsi.

Between corporate spin doctors and constant news coverage, it can be hard to determine the winners of these competitions. It is not like sports where the terms of victory are far more concrete. In the retail world, for example, which company is the victor if overall revenues of Company A are just shy of Company B's, but Company A's same store sales increased at a rate greater than that of Company B's? Both CEOs might declare victory, or try to do so. Which one is right? Over the long term, these ambiguities tend to disappear, as the constancy of superior team performance weeds out the winners from the losers.

In 1978, Arthur Blank and Bernie Marcus were fired from their positions at Handy Dan Home Improvement Centers. According to the book *Inside Home Depot: How One Company Revolutionized an Industry*:

> The day after the firing, Marcus called former Handy Dan investor Ken Langone, who laughed. "Bernie, you just got hit in the rear with a golden horseshoe and don't even know it," said Langone. "You always told me about this dream of a huge store and great service and low prices. Let's do it." Langone agreed to raise $2 million to start Home Depot. Langone liked the way Marcus and Blank treated their employees.
>
> And because Marcus and Blank actively seek out employees who can think and make decisions, they treat them better than other retailers. "You cannot build a vision if you don't have the people who will accept that vision and carry that vision on," says Marcus. "We wanted to surround ourselves with people who felt as we do, who think as we do, who believed what we believed in. You have to believe in yourself and what the vision is. When you believe in something strongly enough, then the dream becomes a fact." Enough employees believe in Marcus and Blank and the Home Depot philosophy. Virtually every one of them calls the cofounders by the first names Bernie and Arthur, because they feel they're just as important to Home Depot's success as are the cofounders and leaders.[16]

Though it is not mentioned directly, pride has played a very important role in the building of the Home Depot team. Marcus and Blank sought employees who would take pride in what they were trying to accomplish and turn dreams into reality.

In 1979, Blank and Marcus launched the first three Home Depot stores in Atlanta, fiddled with the formula for "about nine months" to get it right, then opened a fourth that worked as well as they had hoped. In 1981, Home Depot became a publicly owned company. By 1999, revenues reached $38 billion. The next year, Arthur Blank handed over his CEO position to Robert Nardelli; at the time the company had 250,000 employees, or associates as they were called. Blank has since purchased the Atlanta Falcons professional football team.

The following are excerpts from our conversation with Blank on the benefits gained from building a strong team. He elaborates on and reemphasizes points already discussed. He also introduces new ideas and places a focus on the important role pride plays in motivating teams.

In his own words: Arthur Blank

"BERNIE AND I tried to make a difference in people's lives. Probably one of our strengths at Home Depot was to really get our associates to understand and buy into the culture of our company, which was primarily based on the concept that we were in the business of building—in a very general and broad sense—people's self-confidence . . .

"If you walk into someone's house, the first thing they show you is not what they bought, it's what they did. The whole notion [of the company] is to help people build confidence in themselves, make their headaches go away and make their dreams come true. That was very much the key part of our philosophy. We believed our associates were not the spokes of the wheel, but that they were the cogs of the wheel; they were at the middle of everything we did.

"Associates translated our values system to the customer, and thus the customer felt like they were always in a safe harbor when they were shopping inside our store—that they always felt cared about. It wasn't about the size of the transaction; it had to do with the relationship. If you could make their problem go away or their dream come true for $5 this time, in the future—when they wanted to spend $5,000—then they would come back. . . .

"That is what we worked to have our associates understand . . . that this concept drove the company. We asked our associates to focus on the relationships, on the human side of the equation. By doing this, we realized and enjoyed strong financial results.

"A big part of the joy for me was talking to our associates and seeing, firsthand, the pride they felt in their work, knowing they were making a difference in peoples' lives by providing an important service—watching beautifully wrapped and aggressively priced products come to life as they moved from the shelf to the hands of the customer. Witnessing our customers' joy and fulfillment was an essential part of what drove me and what drove our company for many, many years."

Listening to Blank, one quickly recognizes that the Home Depot associates behave as any well-built team should. Blank and Marcus were successful because, like Beals, Sloan, Thyssen, Jones and many others, they shared their responsibilities with others. While the message always came from them, the associates were the near 300,000 touch points that carried out the message and delivered the experience Blank and Marcus envisioned to millions of customers. Those customers returned to Home Depot not because of Blank, but because of the teams in place at the stores.

Clearly, the company was larger than the two people at the top. But more than that, what really excited Blank was the fact that these teams were effective because the associates took pride in what they did every day, changing people's lives by giving them the self-confidence to excel at something that they may never have tried before.

Continuing on these themes, Blank comments, "I would ask our management team whether this company was worthy of their lives. Because it wasn't just a job. It wasn't just coming to work and working eight, ten, twelve, fourteen hours a day, whatever it would take. I wanted to know if they felt they were part of a system that was bigger than they were and that they were making a difference in the lives of other people.

"If you go back and talk to our associates at Home Depot, they really felt that way. I remember McKinsey did a study for a book on human relations within businesses . . . and after interviewing many others at Home Depot the author saw me. He was in his seventies then and had been doing this for many years, and he said that it was amazing to him, that he went to many of our stores and asked salespersons or cashiers to tell him about the values of this company, and, in every case, it was almost as though he were talking to me or my partner.

"These people, although they phrased it differently, said essentially the same things about their roles in the company, the role of the company in improving customers' lives and how important they were in that whole process."

The obvious question, of course, is how Blank and Marcus built such strong teams. In answering, Blank relates this story. An investment banker once told Blank and Marcus that that the company was reaching the point in its evolution—sales were just shy of $1 billion—where they would be unable to preserve the company's culture, and the effectiveness of the teams would begin to wane.

As Blank remembers, "We dealt with this challenge by making the key criteria for promoting somebody—whether it be to an officer or store manager or district manager or an assistant manager in a store—the following: did they understand the culture of this company? Did they live the culture? Did they believe in it? It wasn't whether they were the best merchant or the best operator or the best whatever they may be. It was about understanding the culture and living it. Would this individual be the evangelist for what we had built for so many years? That was the price to get into the ballpark, if you will. If they understood that and lived it, then we would look at the best merchants, the best operators."

Clearly, Blank believed that pride was an important part of the effectiveness of the Home Depot team. When he promoted people he focused first on how well they grasped the requirements of the new position or how well they performed in previous assignments. What was most important to him was how they felt doing the job. He wanted to know if they had embraced the philosophy of the company. In Blank's mind, Home Depot would only succeed as a result of people placing value in what they did. That sentiment was best displayed if they took pride in and lived the principles espoused by Blank and Marcus.

* * *

Like so many others, Mary Kay Ash, founder of Mary Kay, Inc., saw her company's growth as a result of many people's hard work, especially her sales teams. And like Arthur Blank, she made her company's teams more effective by instilling in them a sense of pride.

Mary Kay, Inc., which has been around for more than forty years, is the number-two direct seller of beauty products in the United States with sales in excess of $1.5 billion. There are many reasons for its success, but none are more important than the thousands of women who serve as independent sales consultants and members of larger sales teams. More than Mary Kay Ash herself, the women representing it are the face of the company. Their success and effectiveness are tied to the incentive programs—such as the pink

Cadillacs—that have been in place since very near the beginning. But more important than any new car or trip around the world is the pride the women feel as a result of working for the company.

For many years, and for many women, Mary Kay, Inc., has represented a woman's right to be independent and to have her own life. For proof, one need look no further than the testimonials of the employees and Ash herself. Lynda Rose, a vice president of Sales and Marketing for the company, says that while the company is in the business of selling beauty products, its greatest impact is the "evolution of a woman." [17]

Speaking to a reporter in 1986, Ash commented that there was no way a woman was ever going to be fairly treated in a business that was run by men. "You have to understand that this was twenty-two years ago. A woman walked two paces behind a man, and there was no way you were going to get into the executive suite.

"You were in the wrong body and that was that. I wanted to create a company that would make it possible for a woman, even a woman with young children, to control how she runs her business." [18]

By providing women with the opportunity to make cold hard cash, often as much as their husbands, the company gave them the self-confidence and self-esteem that many of them never had or might have lost. Mary Kay, Inc., gave women the opportunity to lay claim to an identity independent of their husband's or family's. Satisfied with these new roles, the women, and some men, worked hard not only to perpetuate but also to expand them. As a result, the sales teams became more successful, and in the process, Mary Kay, Inc., grew and prospered.

Most adults must work for a living. But there is a world of difference between working only for a paycheck versus being able to earn a living *and* feel that you are making a difference, as the examples of the sales teams at Mary Kay, Inc., and the associates of Home Depot teach us.

There is no doubt that leaders can coax better work, more energy and greater pride from people who perceive a larger purpose surrounding the team to which they belong. In some cases—such as when a leader heads a nonprofit organization—this purpose is obvious. In other cases, it is up to the leader to nurture such a perception.

History provides us with numerous examples of leaders who accomplished great feats by building a sense of pride within "team" members.

Remember Churchill's speech to the House of Commons just prior to the Battle of Britain? How much more effective were the people of Britain in finding their resolve when what was being asked of them was put in the terms of a higher purpose? In the 16th century, Catherine the Great appealed to the pride of her court to push Russia into the Age of Enlightenment. Pride was the fuel fed by the emperors of feudal Japan to the samurai. Never would the warrior class cower in the face of a threat, so afraid they were of dishonoring themselves before their patrons: "To die without accomplishing one's objectives," they thought, "was to die like a dog." [19]

• • •

All leaders need to acknowledge the importance of team building. The investment will pay dividends for years—whether in terms of growth or survival. In fact, the commitment to building a team and the results that follow are what often distinguish leadership from management. Managers execute; leaders inspire.

A team's destiny is often not immediately apparent. Team building is an ongoing process, during which leaders must show discipline and patience. Only over the course of time, after facing challenges and adversity, will a team be able to demonstrate its true effectiveness. Human resource consultant Michael Thompson observed the following about the 2003 Tour de France:

> The Tour de France is like a mini-business cycle. In spite of the best plans, unforeseen circumstances can force a change in tactics—but not in the ultimate goal. Tyler Hamilton of the CSC team fractured his collarbone early in the race. In spite of tremendous pain, he continued on to support his teammates. On the 16th stage, Tyler fell behind the *peloton*. His team fell back of the main field and pulled Tyler back into the race. That effort enabled Tyler to go on to win the stage. When he won, he acknowledged the team was responsible for the victory, not his individual contribution. This year's tour highlighted numerous examples of team members sacrificing individual glory for the benefit of the team. . . .
>
> Leaders set the goals and take people with them. In the Tour, leaders demonstrate confidence and rise to the occasion. Tyler Hamilton's team could have given up after their star was injured, but their leader's commitment was an inspiration to them all. Leaders must

set the agenda and the tone for the team, inspire commitment, accept accountability, and share success.[20]

Being the head of a team doesn't mean using the team for your own purposes; it means accepting responsibility to bring out the best in the team—at the individual level as well as the group level.

Steven Sample, president of the University of Southern California, writes about the lesson George Clements, noted civil rights leader and religious figure, gave him as he was taking on a new post at the Illinois Board of Higher Education in 1971:

> You should spend a small amount of your time hiring your direct reports, evaluating them, exhorting them, setting their compensation, praising them, kicking their butts and, when necessary, firing them. When you add all that up, it should come out to about 10 percent of your time. For the remaining 90 percent of your time you should be doing everything you can to help your direct reports succeed. You should be the first assistant to the people who work for you."[21]

While not every leader may apply this exact allocation of time, our profiles have shown that many outstanding leaders agree in principle. Harley-Davidson's Beals attended meetings, saying nothing, just as a sign of support of his managers. Blank did everything in his power to make sure that his associates and managers knew that he was available to them, going so far as to request that they refer to him by his first name. By trusting others and offering them the authority to make important decisions, Thyssen, Sloan, and Jones helped their direct reports succeed by making available to them real-world lessons that had real consequences.

The willingness to help others succeed and the ability to develop a strong team assure so many things. We've addressed briefly two of the most important. Teams enable companies and organizations to achieve far more than the sum of individual contribution. Teams also free a company from the limitations of any one person. Effective teams maintain a company's core values and related behaviors when leadership changes or other disruptive events occur.

John Pepper, former chairman and CEO of Procter & Gamble, knows the importance of team building. The company is regarded for its great cohesiveness

Recipe for Glue

No magic wand or silver bullet exists for enduring teamwork. But there might be a recipe, as offered by the consultant David Noer and borrowed by countless others:

> Fill glue pot with the fresh, pure,
> clear water of undiluted human spirit.
>
> Take special care not to contaminate
> with preconceived ideas, or to pollute
> with excess control.
>
> Fill slowly; notice that the pot only fills
> from the bottom up. It's impossible to fill it from
> the top down.
>
> Stir in equal parts of customer focus and pride in good
> work. Bring to a boil and blend in a liberal portion of
> diversity, one part self-esteem, and one part tolerance.
>
> Fold in accountability.
>
> Simmer until smooth and thick, stirring with shared
> leadership and clear goals.
>
> Season with a dash of humor and a pinch of adventure.
>
> Let cool, then garnish with a topping of core values.

Serve by coating all boxes in the organizational chart, paying particular attention to the white spaces. With proper application, the boxes disappear and all that can be seen is productivity, creativity, and customer service.

—David Noer, "Recipe for Glue"[22]

and ability to work in highly effective teams. Pepper says that teamwork is more important than ever before, given the increasing complexity of competing on a global level. P&G has 98,000 employees, marketing almost 300 products to more than five billion consumers in 140 countries.

Pepper told us that for him, a team is made more effective if mentorship is encouraged within it. "Mentorship," he explains, "is important for several reasons. One, when a mentor conveys respect and trust in another person, it tells the other person that they matter.

"It's important, obviously, that the mentor possesses valuable knowledge and is a person that you naturally respect. However, in addition to the teaching or transfer of content and knowledge, it's also about 'How are you doing?' Or 'Here's something you're doing and you may not know it.' You can communicate certain things that may be considered 'critical' because they know you want to help them. Sometimes they might wish that what you were saying wasn't true, but they can accept it and use it to become better."

John A. Luke Jr., chairman and CEO of MeadWestvaco, is also an advocate of mentoring others, saying, "Mentoring is critical if you are going to build an organization that has the capacity to achieve an ambitious vision. A good leader must be able to teach or mentor others and instill in them appreciation of the importance of continual learning. It is important to focus on both the development of the business as well as the development of leadership capabilities.

"Mentoring does this. It's not just about giving leadership direction, it's really helping people understand, on a continuing basis, how they can contribute to a successful venture. It's been my greatest reward to see people succeed at what they do and, in succeeding, to have a heightened level of confidence in knowing what they can achieve."

Mentoring relationships bring talented people into the heart of a team, giving them not just the skills, but also the confidence necessary for them, the team and the company to succeed.

• • •

While few would disagree that a team can accomplish more than an individual in all but the rarest of situations, it is nevertheless surprising how difficult true, effective team building is and, therefore, how often team building efforts fail. Many executives who view themselves as leaders and who would tell you they nourish a teamlike environment are true emperors without clothing. The reasons for this are many, not the least of which is the fact that most of us are taught to make decisions rather than to delegate. We take it upon ourselves to provide direction and feel that as "the leader" we are expected to know what to do and direct others to get it done. True leading, however, is not about telling; it is about inspiring.

More relevant, however, is the disconnect between an executive's message and his or her behavior. As the hierarchical model of management has been replaced with matrix models and centralized decision making is being decentralized, many organizations went "back to school" to learn how to build teams. Millions of dollars have been spent on training, development, and communications designed to teach executives and the rank and file alike how to be effective team players. Often the training builds an expectation of behavioral change that is never met. For example, "bad behavior" on the part of key people is not addressed. Executives talk teamwork, but walk alone. The troops on the other hand expect too much too soon or are not willing to move out of the comfort-zone rut—where people express a desire for more accountability but are not willing to take some of the risks more accountability implies, finding it easier to blame management.

"How do you recognize if a team is good? It's simple," says Harry Kraemer, CEO of Baxter International. It begins with the idea that the members of the team are trying hard, not to be right but to do the right thing.

"A team that really works well together is one where there are no sidebar conversations. People aren't going over to the soda machine during breaks and saying to each other, 'Can you believe . . .' Everything is so open and seamless that comments are made during the middle of the meeting.

"When you get to that point, that's how you know you've got a great team, because everyone is focused on doing the right thing. Everyone is paying attention to the team rather than themselves or making somebody else look bad."

A leader's track record can be a major indicator of his or her ability to build teams. Yet this is an area where many are eloquent in their expression but deficient in their execution. There are, however, a number of ways that indicate how capable a leader is at building teams.

First, looking at other traits affords us the opportunity to better examine this one:

+ *Self-confidence*: The need to control is the greatest inhibitor of sharing responsibility. Individuals with a high degree of self-confidence are better able to share authority; those who suffer from insecurities will, particularly when the heat is on, resort to autonomy and directive behavior.

- *Listening*: Listening is tied to self-confidence. It will be addressed in detail in Chapter 7, but suffice it to say here that those who understand—and accept—that they will never know enough to make decisions on their own appreciate what they can learn from others and listen more effectively.

- *Heart*: As discussed in the previous chapter, those who lead with their hearts seem to have a greater capacity to care about others' feelings and others' needs. Leaders with heart are inclined to lead holistically and care deeply about the contribution others are able to make for the greater good.

- *Diversity*: As we will cover in the final chapter and as alluded to early on in this chapter, surrounding oneself with a diverse group of opinions, perspectives, and levels of experience will provide leaders with the most robust set of perspectives they need to lead. Inherent in cultivating diversity is the notion of sharing ownership, leveraging common values, and appreciating differences.

Second, how well a person answers questions relating to the experience of forming a team tells us much about their abilities to execute. How did the team come together? Did they inherit the team or did they pick it? It is important for us to know their style in putting a team together. It is also important for us to know how a leader relates to a team and how decisions are made within the group. Was it a collaborative environment or dictatorial one? Knowing these things gives us a better understanding of what type of leader the person we are talking to is.

Third, how thoroughly an executive embraces team building is often revealed by subtle language cues. The best team builders, the ones who execute, speak in terms of "we" rather than "I." When they talk about loyalty, they do not focus on the team's loyalty to them, but instead on their loyalty to the team.

A perspective from the Russell Reynolds Associates Executive Assessment Team

Leadership exists in the eyes and perceptions of followers. Without followers, leadership by definition could not exist. Even if an individual has all of the leadership traits—vision, tenacity, strategic and tactical thinking, and so on, that person cannot be successful unless he or she can assemble and motivate a team to carry out the vision. To do this effectively, it is imperative that leaders attract and develop a diversity of individuals for their teams and appeal to individuals with varied personalities, cultures, professional backgrounds, and work styles.

In building a team, it is important to select individuals who share the organization's values but offer a diversity of skills and approaches to achieving the organization's goals. Thus, a leader who seeks to find team members who share his or her training, experiences and thinking style may later find the organization stagnant and unable to grow or creatively solve problems. Rather, by selecting a team of individuals who can approach a problem or a strategic dilemma from varying perspectives, a team will benefit from a variety of innovative ideas as well as having a productive dialogue about possible solutions.

Successful leaders understand four basic tenets about team building:

First, managing the behavior of a team is different than managing the behavior of individuals. To manage the performance of a team effectively, the leader needs to take into account other factors that affect performance such as the environment in which the team works, the interdependency of individuals' work on the team and the reward system. For example, to foster cooperation rather than competition between team members, it is crucial that the organization provide rewards that reinforce a cooperative team system.

Second, team performance is an interaction rather than a sum. Therefore, having only creative individuals on a team does not ensure creativity. Effective team leaders know that it is imperative to have individuals with diverse skills and talents balance out the weaknesses in one another. Just as diversification is important in putting together a financial investment portfolio, leaders must invest in a diversity of people to have a team that can be effective against different landscapes over time.

Third, teams need different kinds of leadership at different stages in their development. While a top-line approach may be appropriate for leading teams at the entrepreneurial stage, a structuring approach may be more effective in an implementation stage. Truly effective leaders are able to adapt their behaviors based on the current business needs in order to most effectively guide their teams while providing a consistent vision and modeling their values to their teams on a daily basis.

Fourth, effective leaders recognize the importance of communication in managing teams. Communication is key to clearly implementing a vision and establishing consistency for individuals who may be working separately toward the same goal. For example, it is important that individuals on a global team understand the unified goals of their team and communicate using a common jargon. In addition, it is important that individuals understand the priorities of the team and what their individual responsibility to the project is. Clear communication on this issue will pave the way for accountability and will provide individuals with an understanding of how their roles fit into the big picture.

Leaders who build teams successfully reap many benefits. Individuals who are part of a team often feel more invested in the outcome of high-priority goals and feel less pressure to carry the weight of important initiatives on their own. In addition, teams consisting of members with diverse skills and talents often have higher-quality brainstorms around ideas and greater checks and balances in processes. Functionally interdependent teams often have more commitment and endurance to put toward challenging and time-sensitive goals. Finally, teams are often efficient as well as effective. Teams can share resources, responsibilities and knowledge. Thus, the benefits of building teams can be realized at both the top-line ideas and visions and the bottom-line interests of the organization.

sources

1. Selected quote, "Teamwork," http://www.industryweek.com/Columns/ASP/ columns.asp?ColumnId=545 (accessed February 15, 2004).

2. Selected quote, "Teamwork," http://217.11.110.254/search/author.asp?id=5056&page=5 (accessed February 15, 2004).

3. David A. Moss, "The Deutshe Bank," in *Creating Modern Capitalism: How Entrepreneurs, Companies, and Countries Triumphed in Three Industrial Revolutions,* ed. Thomas K. McCraw, (Cambridge, MA: Harvard University Press, 1997), p. 233.

4. The three banks that stayed with Harley-Davidson were paid back in full; only Citicorp Industrial Credit took a discount to get out (12/31/85).

5. This concept for H.O.G was based on the homespun philosophy of the late Charlie Thompson (COO of the company from 1981 to 1982) that "if a motorcycle sits in the garage too long, it turns into furniture." In other words, it's essential to get your spouse involved in the sport. Unfortunately, in early 1982, when things were at their worst at Harley-Davidson, Charlie had a heart attack and shortly thereafter a transplant. Although he was unable to practice his own philosophy, he maintained his role as an advisor.

6. Selected quote, "Teamwork," http://www.wisdomquotes.com/cat_leadership.html (accessed February 15, 2004).

7. Jeffrey Bleustein, "Remarks," speech at the Summit on the 21st Century Workforce, Washington, D.C., June 20, 2001), http://www.dol.gov/21cw/speeches/jeffrey_bluestein.htm (accessed February 22, 2004).

8. A Konzern is a multisubsidiary institution. Within it, a parent company sets the financial and strategic course of legally independent subordinate firms.

9. Jeffrey Fear, "August Thyssen and German Steel," in *Creating Modern Capitalism*, p. 189.

10. Ibid., p. 192.

11. Thomas K. McCraw and Richard S. Tedlow, "Henry Ford, Alfred Sloan, and the Three Phases of Marketing," in *Creating Modern Capitalism*, p. 287.

12. Ibid.

13. James C. Collins and Porras, *Built to Last: Successful Habits of Visionary Companies* (New York: HarperBusiness, 1994), p. 170.

14. Jack Welch, with John A. Byrne, *Jack: Straight from the Gut* (New York: Warner Books, 2001), p.34.

15. Ibid., p. 59

16. Chris Roush, *Inside Home Depot: How One Company Revolutionized an Industry* (New York: McGraw-Hill Companies, 1999).

17. *National Post* (Canada), "Mary Kay: Before she became a cosmetics giant, Mary Kay Ash had a rather simple plan by today's standards—to give women an equal opportunity to succeed," July 30, 2003.

18. Anne V. Hull, "Mary Kay: Talk Softly and Carry a Big Shtick," *St. Petersburg Times* (Florida), February 1, 1987.

19. Kiyoharu Omino, introduction to *Samurai Sketches: From the Bloody Final Years of the Shogun*, by Romulous Hillsborough (Pinole, CA: Ridgeback Press, 2001).

20. Michael A. Thompson, "What Leaders Can Learn from the Tour de France, "Mercer Human Resource Consulting, www.mercerhr.com/knowledgecenter/home.jhtml/ dynamic/ topicId/117000000/geographyId/-1?topicId= (accessed February 22,2004).

21. Selected quote, "Teamwork," http://www.brainyquote.com/quotes/authors/l/lao_tzu.html (accessed February 15, 2004).

22. Steven B. Sample, *The Contrarian's Guide to Leadership* (San Francisco: Jossey-Bass, 2002).

23. David Noer, "Recipe for Glue," Noer Consulting, http://www.noerconsulting.com/recipe.html (accessed February 24, 2004).

6

Backbone

Fall seven times, stand up eight.
—Japanese proverb[1]

Fate gave to man the courage of endurance.
—Ludwig van Beethoven[2]

SOMETIMES IT TAKES MORE than vision, voice or any of the other traits described thus far in this book. There are some challenges that are so overwhelmingly difficult that the most compelling trait a leader requires to succeed is an unusual ability to persevere.

Perseverance or "backbone" is a trait important to most enduring leaders.

We find that those leaders who display a strong backbone are often misunderstood. People may see them as unaffected by the adversity and anguish that challenges can bring.

However, they are human, and they feel pain just like the rest of us. But they do not let that stop them.

What many people know about Marjorie Scardino is that she is the CEO of Pearson plc, and that she has been recognized by *Fortune* magazine as the most powerful woman in business outside the United States. What is not so well known is that early in her married life, she and her husband used their personal savings to revive a weekly newspaper in Savannah, Georgia.

While winning high marks, including a 1984 Pulitzer Prize, the *Georgia Gazette* was never able to make much money, despite Scardino's hard work as its business manager. Thus, when the county pulled its advertising from the paper, the Scardinos had no choice but to fold the paper; they were left with a $250,000 debt.[3]

A failure of the type that Marjorie Scardino and her husband experienced would cripple many of us, especially when it comes accompanied by such a large debt. But Scardino did not let it derail her ambitions. She was able to leverage her experience at the newspaper to her advantage. Contacting recruiters in New York afterward, she did not dwell on the negative aspects of the experience, but instead promoted her time working at the paper with a maxim that she has since oft repeated: "You learn more from failure than you do from success."[4] (Or, as Henry Ford said, "Failure is the only opportunity to begin again more intelligently.")[5]

Executives at the Economist Group believed her and appointed Scardino managing director of North America. As David Gordon, then CEO of the Economist Group, recalled: "My view was that she had extraordinary human qualities and talent. Besides, she had had one of those searing experiences that either makes or breaks you."[6]

As we now know, Scardino was in fact made by her experience running that small Georgia newspaper. And, as a result, many have been able to benefit.

•　　•　　•

Harlan Sanders, that genteel old gentleman whose face has long adorned the Kentucky Fried Chicken franchise, was not an immediate success. For Sanders, success came late in life, well after he passed the age of sixty.

Starting work at the age of ten, Sanders had at least eight careers during his lifetime. He did not actually begin to cook for people until he was forty, and that was only to attract customers to his service station in Corbin,

Kentucky. People liked what they ate and soon that service station became a motel and a restaurant.

Unfortunately, in the early 1950s, a highway's development caused Sanders to close his businesses. After auctioning off his operations and paying his bills, he was left to live off his $105 Social Security checks. At the time, he was sixty-two years old.[7] For many of us, that is where our story would end. But for Sanders, it was just a setback and certainly not an insurmountable one

Confident that he had something with his chicken recipe, Sanders sought a way to make his restaurant business stick. He concluded the answer was in franchising and started what would be his last career. Traveling across the country from restaurant to restaurant, he tried to convince restaurant owners of the merits of his fried chicken. His secret formula was rejected over a thousand times before its potential was finally seen.[8] And seen it was. By 1964, Harlan "Colonel" Sanders had more than six hundred franchised Kentucky Fried Chicken outlets in the United States and Canada.[9]

● ● ●

Milton Hershey, he of chocolate-bar fame, began his career in printing. When that soon ended, he apprenticed as a confectioner. By the age of nineteen, Hershey was operating his own candy manufacturing business in Philadelphia. By the age of twenty-five, he was looking for work.

Hershey tried to make candy in Denver, then Chicago, New Orleans, and finally New York. The results, however, were the same in those places as they were in Philadelphia. Despite knowing how to make all types of candy, Hershey simply could not run a successful business. So he returned home to Lancaster, Pennsylvania.

A friend lent him some money and Hershey used it to start, of all things, a candy business. With the help of his mother and aunt, he set out to build another candy company, focusing on only one product—caramels.

Fate finally found Milton Hershey in the form of a visiting Englishman who happened to be a candy importer. This man tasted one of Hershey's caramels and immediately fell in love. He wanted large quantities to be shipped to England. Suddenly Hershey was successful. So successful, in fact, that Hershey's candies—there would soon be over one hundred types—were sold in places as far away as China and Australia, requiring the business to expand to New York and Chicago.

The company we are all so familiar with did not begin until Hershey sold his caramel business. The $1 million he received from the American Caramel Company was used to finance a new factory, which was dedicated solely to the production of chocolate.[10]

· · ·

We began this chapter with brief mention of the stories of three very different people who all share one trait in common—each has displayed perseverance or backbone.

Marjorie Scardino, Harlan Sanders, and Milton Hershey stayed true to their dreams and ambitions, even when the world seemed to be working against them. We view each of these people as outstanding and effective leaders. Each showed a tenacity that drove them to press ahead, even in the face of adversity.

Life is not easy. There are major showstoppers such as debt, opposition, and bad luck. For many of these obstacles to be overcome, a leader needs more than a vision, and he or she must be more than a good communicator and listener. A leader has to want something so badly and believe enough in his or her own abilities to be willing to face and overcome the seemingly infinite challenges that may stand in the way. In some ways, backbone is like a trait talked about earlier—not wanting to live a small life. It makes a leader effective solely by its existence. It does not need to involve others.

> I have not failed. I've just found 10,000 ways that won't work.
> —Thomas Alva Edison[11]

Someone who understands the value of perseverance better than most is Shelly Lazarus, chairman and CEO of the advertising agency Ogilvy & Mather. She spoke with us about Ogilvy losing the American Express account and what it took to get the agency's seminal client back.

In her own words: Shelly Lazarus

"LOSING AMERICAN EXPRESS was absolutely devastating to me because I had worked on that business for so long. And while I was working in another division when it happened, I was called back to see if the relationship could be salvaged. I knew, almost immediately, that it couldn't be saved.

"I didn't tell anybody, but I knew these clients well enough to see they had lost faith. Even more importantly, the people in the agency had lost faith. They didn't think they could come up with a solution that the American Express people would believe in.

"In the end, the client took all the sexy parts of the assignment away, like the brand advertising. But it did leave us with the little stuff that the other agency wasn't interested in, which was basically the service establishment piece of the business. As such, we had this very small, unsexy piece of the business. The question was how to handle it."

Lazarus's first decision came the next day, when Citibank called to ask her if Ogilvy would be interested in doing its advertising. If she accepted, the lost American Express revenue would be restored, but she would also have to resign the small bit of business American Express left to Ogilvy. Lazarus considered but then declined Citibank's offer, despite the fact that it made more business sense.

Explaining her decision, Lazarus says, "[American Express] was an integral part of who we were, and I couldn't bring myself to walk away from them. What we were most famous for, what had established us in the industry, was what we had done for them. And because American Express is so brand based, what we had done for them built their business. We were too important to each other's histories, I think, for me to turn my back on them for good."

Once she turned down Citibank, Lazarus made her second most important decision. "I resolved to make whatever work we were given by [American Express] the best work we could do. Whatever it took—no matter the period of time—we were going to win them back. It was a leap of faith on my part, but I thought we understood this brand better than anybody and that our intimate brand understanding would take us back to American Express."

It is in this decision that Lazarus reveals her backbone. No matter how small Ogilvy's share of the American Express business was relative to the whole, there was nothing that would prevent it from reclaiming the lion's share of the account. She was determined that the agency would prove itself with the quality of its product and would continue to prove itself until there were no more challenges to overcome.

"Making this decision was easy," Lazarus says. "What was more challenging was getting other people to take on the challenge with me, because they were hurt, they were angry, they were mad. They had been publicly humiliated.

They were frustrated. And so this was a great management challenge, to gather a group of people who would be able to persevere like I wanted them to, like I was willing to do."

In the end, Lazarus had to recruit a new group of people to work on the account. She recalls fondly, "It turned out to be a real labor of love. We just put our noses to the grindstone, and we did what we were asked to do beyond expectations. And we got it back in ten months; ten months is all it took."

By persevering, Lazarus was able to win back American Express. But the drive she exhibited in doing so was nothing new to those who have worked with her through the years. In fact, that determination to not be beaten by a challenge is something that made Lazarus, and by extension Ogilvy & Mather, attractive to IBM.

When Lou Gerstner, who had worked with Lazarus while at American Express, took over the leadership at IBM, he recognized that in order to fix IBM, its brand image had to be fixed. He believed that Ogilvy was the agency most capable of dealing with the challenges of such a monumental task because it would not be intimidated by the challenges, nor would it give up prior to finding an effective solution.

The IBM brand, says Lazarus, was "totally fragmented as a result of the previous leadership's efforts to try to unleash the entrepreneurial energies of the company. There was no cohesion. Each division was on its own, able to choose how or whether it would leverage the company's name.

"If IBM were to correct itself in a reasonable period of time, [Gerstner] had to find a way to get everything back together. To do that quickly, and with some control, he was going to have to work with one agency, because he just didn't have time to tell forty-five agencies what needed to be done.

"I think in the end the feeling was that [Gerstner] was going to pick people who he had worked with before and had been successful with before. Because he knew how we worked, he trusted us."

Thus, Gerstner chose Lazarus and Ogilvy. Having seen firsthand how the agency and its executive officer did not cower in the face of challenges, he knew that they were the ones who would most effectively articulate IBM's new brand identity. So IBM fired the forty-five agencies then working for it and gave all of its advertising work to Ogilvy & Mather. The tenacity Lazarus and her colleagues had shown over the years engendered Gerstner's belief that they were prepared to facing the pending trials.

After the vast majority of the account was lost, few would have questioned Lazarus if she had decided to abandon American Express entirely to focus her firm's attention elsewhere. She did not do that, because she was confident that if Ogilvy continued to work hard for American Express, it would again reap dividends.

In order to press ahead, leaders must believe that they will be successful. Desire only lasts for so long. To continually meet challenges, desire must be augmented by the belief that one will succeed. If that belief or confidence does not exist, eventually even the most passionate will give up and turn their attentions elsewhere.

Jay Fishman, CEO of St. Paul Travelers (formerly chairman, president, and CEO of the St. Paul Companies, Inc.), spoke to us about the relationship between knowledge and perseverance. He believes that few leaders will persevere if they are not in possession of a deep understanding of what they are fighting for.

"The confidence I'm talking about comes from nothing more than good analysis. I believe, fundamentally, that many decisions—good decisions—are the result of thoughtful, meaningful analysis. Quality work is less instinctive than you might think. Ultimately, it is the analysis that you do that leads one to the conviction of one's belief.

"And I'm not talking about analyzing something to the nth degree. There is an opportunity to scrutinize most issues; on many of them, the answer becomes obvious, if the analysis is thoughtful and proper. From all of that comes the sense of knowing you're going to succeed." Fishman went on to cite an instance when he used analysis as support for remaining true to his convictions and persevering, despite other people's best efforts to get him to acquiesce.

"There was a particular acquisition that I was charged to work on. From both my perspective and the quality of my due diligence, the transaction made no sense, and in fact, would result in a problem if we were to go with it. However, it was something that other people really wanted to do. There was a perspective, I think, that perhaps I was being too harsh or that I didn't have enough vision to see the value in it. From a distance, it seemed to be a terrific fit, and it made a lot of sense.

"Despite the pressure I was feeling, my analysis told me what was right. I stood my ground, even though I might have been better off personally if I backed down a bit. Ultimately, we didn't do the transaction, and the company we were going to acquire ended up in bankruptcy."

Analysis and hard work provided Fishman with the confidence necessary to stand behind a course that was by no means popular. He knew that by remaining true to his convictions, he was jeopardizing some of his professional relationships, but the result was the continued health of the company.

•   •   •

We often think that leaders who show backbone are different than the rest of us. They do not feel the same frustration when encountering a challenge; nor do they feel the same sense of pain or rejection when they fail. So often do they carry on in the face of overwhelming obstacles that we are left in awe and wonder at how they do it. But leaders do feel the pain an vulnerability that "normal" people feel when having failed.

When anyone develops a deadly form of cancer, it is devastating. But when that person is only twenty-four years old, in a profession that requires perfect conditioning, it is also the end of a lifetime of dreams. This is the situation that confronted American cyclist Lance Armstrong.

As many know, Armstrong survived, returned to his bike and won the Tour de France not once or twice, but five times in a row. His victories were not just over other great athletes, they were over his deadly disease.

What many do not know is that in 1998, after beating incredible odds and recovering, Armstrong returned to the professional cycling circuit and competed in the Paris-Nice race. The weather was absolutely miserable, and Armstrong pulled out in Stage 2, believing he had given his best shot and lost, not only in the race, but also in his attempt to return to competitive racing.

His fiancée, Kristen (now his ex-wife), wrote at the time:

Something profound is happening here. Something that perhaps only those who have personally recovered from an intense battle with cancer can understand. It is only beginning to reveal itself to Lance. The thing I'm referring to is a powerful transition. At the time when Lance pulled over in Paris-Nice and we left Europe, we were both too close to the situation to fully comprehend what was happening. Lance felt so unsure about what he was doing and what was motivating him. We took a hiatus so he could re-evaluate.

One morning we had a serious discussion and I carefully approached the subject of "What now?" After giving him his space, I wanted to know what the plan was. He still didn't know. I reminded him that it was not the Armstrong way to let a decision be made by not deciding. He either needed to retire the bike or get back on it with renewed commitment. It was not an easy discussion, but it was an honest one, and he took it to heart. A few days later he was back on the bike with a vengeance. I wonder now, looking back on the past month, if we weren't dealing with something as simple as FEAR.

Everyone experiences it, sometimes it paralyzes and other times it propels. I think on some inner level, Lance was afraid. Afraid of trying. Afraid of failing. Afraid of not living up to his past or to other people's expectations. Afraid that the cancer had taken some of his singular drive and his competitive fire. Afraid that maybe pushing his body that hard again could somehow bring back the cancer. Like a tightrope walker with a fear of heights, he had to relearn how to walk without looking down.[12]

Shortly thereafter, Armstrong spent a week in Boone, North Carolina, the site of a previous victory. In racing up part of the old course—a mountain known to eat bikers alive—Armstrong experienced a rebirth. He discovered the courage and drive that still burned bright within him, and then he started his legendary comeback.

We offer this story of Lance Armstrong as proof that leaders do experience pain and fear. Adversity is not easier for them to take. To the contrary, they are every bit as vulnerable as anyone else.

What sets them apart, however, is that when they look deep inside for extra ounces of reserve to get them through unbelievable challenges, they find more fuel. They keep going when others might quit. What drives those with a strong backbone is the deep desire to accomplish something and the belief that one can do it.

•   •   •

William Foote, chairman, president, and CEO of USG Corporation, is familiar with a story similar to Armstrong's. However, his does not end as well. His first wife lost her battle with cancer. While motivating and helping her during her illness, Foote came to better recognize the inevitability of adversity and began to better demonstrate the tenacity and strength of spirit necessary if one is to overcome a hardship. Eventually, he applied the lessons he learned from his wife's sickness to his professional life, to the challenges that have threatened something else about which he deeply cares: his company.

In his own words: William Foote

"I'VE HAD TWO huge disappointments in my life," says Foote. "One personal and one professional. The personal was the loss of my wife in 1995, just months before I became CEO. My professional disappointment has been the legal obstruction we're in the midst of right now, which is bankruptcy. The challenge is huge because it isn't about our enterprise, but rather it is about the broken legal system of country [the U.S.].

"With regards to the first, I'm very happily remarried. We have five kids—three from my first wife and two with my wife Kari. I've always been an optimist, but necessity has changed that somewhat. Now I have one foot on the optimistic side, and another on the side of reality. It's a better place to be.

"These personal and professional challenges have led me to a more philosophical approach to life. There's nothing like losing your wife or having your company declare bankruptcy. It feels like a cold shower. I'm fifty-three, and I've had two really cold showers. You get tougher and more compassionate at the same time . . . and move on."

As is the case when you talk to any strong leader, what comes out of talking to Foote is his will. It's easy to minimize how overwhelming many of his darkest days must have been, because he refuses to be held down by the cards life has dealt him. He does, however, confess that there are times when the help of others is much appreciated.

When his first wife's illness was diagnosed, he told his team, and they rallied to support him. When she passed away, he gave an emotional speech to some of his colleagues in which, according to the *Wall Street Journal*, he reminded them that life is precious and fleeting. It is important, he urged, to do all you can and never to give up on what really matters: kids, self, family, work.[13]

We asked Foote to give us some background on the factors underlying USG's bankruptcy and the challenges he now faces.

"USG's annual sales are more than $3.5 billion. Our company is best known for Sheetrock brand drywall—in fact, we invented drywall in 1917. We are the largest manufacturer in North America.

"Our market shares are in the mid-30s in drywall and significantly greater than that in joint compound. We're a leader in every single business except in one category in one product family. It's a thriving enterprise. We've got a billion dollars in cash on the balance sheet. We're hardly an enterprise that's not showing signs of health.

"We used asbestos in some of our products, and stopped doing so more than twenty-five years ago. We never mined it or produced it—asbestos was a minor ingredient in some of our joint compounds and plasters. As a result of the arcane rules regarding asbestos litigation, we were bombarded with asbestos lawsuits, even though we were a very minor player compared to other companies. We are one of sixty-seven companies in the past 20 years to file for bankruptcy as a result of asbestos litigation. We are actually one of the strong companies, but we've experienced a domino effect with these lawsuits that has played out in waves.

"The first wave started with Johns-Manville, the company that produced the mineral. The second wave consisted of insulation companies whose products contained asbestos. We're in the third wave now, which includes minor users, like USG. There is another wave coming that will include big companies— Fortune 100 companies. As more companies enter bankruptcy, the lawsuits are redirected at other, nonbankrupt companies, regardless of their actual involvement with asbestos. This problem is not going away."

> Somehow I can't believe there are any heights that can't be achieved by men who know the secret of making dreams come true. This special secret, it seems to me, can be summarized in four C's. They are Curiosity, Confidence, Courage, and Constancy, and the greatest of these is Confidence. When you believe a thing, believe in it all the way.
>
> —Walt Disney[14]

About five years ago, Foote decided that the best hope for his company was to fight for legislative changes that would deal with the health-related consequences of asbestos without destroying companies that are fundamentally healthy, as well as the sources of income for their employees and the communities in which they work. It has been a long, hard, uphill battle.

At first, Foote explains, "We only had a couple of people enthusiastically supporting that legislation. The others were saying, 'Well, we'll never get it done.' They were naysayers, but we have persevered. It remains to be seen whether we will get a new law passed, but we're down in the red zone and there's no one in Washington who doesn't know about this litigation nightmare.

"Some of the largest companies in America are fighting with me to fix the system. It's an example of where we had very long odds and not a lot of support, but we're motivated to do right by our company and do right by America. My motivation has been not only to protect our company, but to also effect good public policy.

"The capital markets are closed for our company right now, not because we don't have a terrific business, but rather because they don't know how deep the problem is and are afraid of the risks.

"A $100+ billion, privately funded trust, backed by industry and by insurance, is under consideration in the U.S. Senate right now. It's been very energizing to work toward this legislation, and whether it passes or not, it is the right thing to do and we will persevere. In the end, our shareholders and our team know that we have played every last card to try and get this done."

● ● ●

History is filled with leaders who, like Foote, understood that to overcome adversity is never to think that one is defeated. Consider the examples of the South American revolutionary Simón Bolívar, and the American caregiver Dorothea Dix.

Bolívar was born in 1783 to a wealthy family in what is now Venezuela. He was sent to Spain when he was fifteen to complete his education. In Europe during the Napoleonic wars, he saw firsthand the tragedy that exists when one country rules another. He vowed that he would not rest until South America was free. Visiting the United States upon his return home in 1811, Bolívar no doubt saw the differences that existed between the newly independent country and the colonies of South America. He took the spirit of the American Revolution home with him and used it as the fuel to drive his own efforts toward independence.

By 1813, Bolívar was leading a small army and had won control of Venezuela. But the next year, he was forced out of the country. For four years,

Bolívar alternated between victories and defeats. Repeatedly his situation seemed hopeless, but he never gave up. Instead, he just sought new ways to overcome the challenges he faced.

Thus, he turned his attention away from Venezuela to what is now Colombia. He led a force of 2,500 men in a march for eleven months across Venezuela, fording seven rivers and climbing the Andes

> I assess the power of a will by how much resistance, pain, torture it endures and knows how to turn to its advantage.
> —Friedrich Wilhelm Nietzsche[15]

to cross into Colombia. Surprising the Spaniards, he defeated them, entering Bogotá on August 10, 1819. Bolívar was hailed as the liberator of Colombia, giving him the power to demand and secure the independence of other countries in the region: Peru, Ecuador, Venezuela, and Bolivia.[16]

Dorothea Dix shared Bolívar's temperament. She was relentless in her efforts to solve a problem that few others bothered to address, tirelessly campaigning to bring medical care to the mentally ill, who during the mid-nineteenth century were often locked in prisons or simply ignored. Reports one account of Dix's life:

> [She] traveled thousands of miles from state to state—by train, coach, carriage and river boat—always systematically gathering facts which she could use to try to convince those in authority of the need of improvement in the care of the mentally ill. After seeing for herself, she would present a "memorial" to the state legislature with her concerns in which she described conditions as she found them.
>
> Dorothea would enter an urgent plea for the establishment of state-supported institutions. She would actively lobby for passage of the bill, looking for sponsors and trying to win over the often large numbers of persons who opposed such legislation. The first state hospital built as a result of her efforts was located at Trenton, New Jersey.
>
> Interrupted by malaria and suffering from poor health, Dorothea continued in her life's ambition of trying to improve the lot of the mentally ill worldwide. In the 1850's she carried on her work in the British Isles, France, Greece, Russia, Canada, Japan and the United States with hospitals being established in those locations.[17]

What Dix did in order to improve the lives of others was astounding, and it is an outstanding illustration of perseverance. First, it was *she* who investigated how the mentally ill were being treated. Then it was *she* who had to convince various legislatures and opposition groups that what she was demanding was in fact something that was right. How many of us would *volunteer*, as she did, to take up such a cause, to be the voice of those no one wanted to hear?

But Dix's story does not end with the work that she put into her cause. So committed was she that neither illness, which at the time could have been fatal, nor logistical barriers would keep her from achieving her goal. Once change began in America, Dix demanded that it happen everywhere. So strong was Dix's will that there were few challenges she would not meet and overcome. She was a leader of large proportion and someone we continue to admire.

●   ●   ●

Different motivations fuel the spirit necessary to stand and face obstacle after obstacle until a goal is met. Some leaders, like Dix and Foote, are driven by a sense of what is right. Personal ambition or a competitive spirit drives others. But to get through difficult times, leaders need a strong foundation of values. They have to know, deep down in their hearts, what they are fighting for or what is important to them.

Rick Menell is chairman of Anglovaal Mining, Ltd., in South Africa. He is the third generation of his family to lead the company, though he came to it at a relatively late date, having spent his younger years overseas, not wanting to join the company.

Menell spoke with us about what made him change his mind and what now enables him to stand up and face the types of challenges that, as a young man, he would most likely give in to.

"I felt that I would never work for the family's business because it carried too much baggage," says Menell. "I felt that it would not serve my personal development because nothing I would ever have done would have been to my credit; it would be something I inherited. I also found it difficult to work in the unjust society that was South Africa."

But when his father got sick and South Africa moved away from apartheid, Menell decided to join the family business. "I felt comfortable coming back when my dad got sick because I felt my personal compass points were in place; the reading I had done and the experience I had had helped me establish a set of ethics and values against which I could measure my life.

"My strengths are to treat people properly, to deal honestly, to use authority wisely. When running an enterprise you must innately under-stand your compass points and use them to settle on the right course of action quickly, even if you are not certain. They equip you to keep on going if something bad or unexpected happens."

Armed with this self-awareness, Menell has been able to make the changes he thinks essential if the South African mining industry is to remain competitive in the future.

"By modernizing and integrating the enterprise, it's again about compass points. A core driving passion for me is to build mines the right way, being a good citizen and making a contribution to the country. I think modernization and integration—we call it empowerment—touch on a lot of that. And because it does, I'm willing to do near anything to overcome whatever opposition these proposals come up against."

Rick Menell has been able to persevere and stand up to repeated challenges because of a strong foundation of values. He does not get defeated because to do so, on some level, would mean that he is turning his back on himself, rejecting the values that he holds so dear.

•   •   •

There are two essential elements inherent to perseverance. First is the confidence of knowing that something can be done. Second is the desire for that something to be realized. Perseverance or backbone is what allows people to accomplish what may have appeared to be impossible.

When industries and companies are built, there is an immense need for confidence and resilience among the architects. This was certainly the case when a struggling firm named Commercial Credit dared to transform itself into Citigroup, the world's largest financial institution. The following is a condensed timeline of Commercial Credit's evolution into Citigroup:

1985   Sanford I. Weill leaves American Express.

1986   Through a public offering, Commercial Credit is spun off
        from Control Data Corporation with Weill as chairman and
        chief executive officer.

1987   Commercial Credit's earnings from continuing operations more than double from $37.4 million in 1986 to $101.5 million in 1987.

1988   Jerry Tsai transforms American Can Company into a financial services company called Primerica Corporation. The prestigious brokerage house of Smith Barney is added to the Primerica family.

1989   Commercial Credit acquires Primerica Corporation, which includes Smith Barney, American Capital Management & Research and A. L. Williams, for $1.5 billion. The parent company adopts the name Primerica Corporation.

1989   Smith Barney acquires 16 offices from Drexel Burnham Lambert, adding more than $100 million in annual commissions.

1990   Commercial Credit acquires the consumer lending operations of BarclaysAmerican/Financial, including 159 branches and $1 billion in receivables.

1992   Primerica Corporation forms a strategic alliance with the Travelers Corporation by investing $722.5 million for a 27 percent interest in the company.

1993   Primerica Corporation acquires the retail brokerage and asset management operations of Shearson Lehman Brothers from American Express and combines them with Smith Barney, creating the second-largest investment banking and brokerage firm in the world. Primerica Corporation purchases the remaining 73 percent of the Travelers Corporation common stock and changes its name to Travelers, Inc.

1998   Travelers Group and Citibank complete their merger. The combined company is called Citigroup.

In 1982, Jamie Dimon was hired out of Harvard Business School to become Sandy Weill's personal assistant at American Express. Dimon stuck by Weill when the latter was forced out of American Express. He later helped Weill acquire and turn Commercial Credit into first, Primerica, then Travelers and finally Citigroup. One month after the Citigroup deal, Dimon's longtime mentor forced him out of the company.

Dimon's career, for the most part, can best be described as "success born from perseverance." He has overcome much, from leaving American Express to his very public departure from the company he helped build. Dimon is now chairman and CEO of Bank One, and pending approval of that company's merger with J.P. Morgan Chase, will soon be president and COO of the merged entity.

We close our discussion on perseverance with selected excerpts from our conversation with Dimon. From his words emerges a multilayered definition of what perseverance means in a business environment.

> If I had to select one quality, one personal characteristic that I regard as being most highly correlated with success, whatever the field, I would pick the trait of persistence. Determination. The will to endure to the end, to get knocked down seventy times and get up off the floor saying, Here comes number seventy-one!
> —Richard M. Devos, founder of Amway[18]

In his own words: Jamie Dimon

SPEAKING OF WHY he stayed with his mentor after Weill was dismissed from American Express, Dimon says, "The easy answer is that I liked and respected [Weill]. But I also wanted to do something that went beyond climbing the corporate ladder. [Weill] was different than the average corporate guy, and we had a very good relationship. At some point, I became convinced that if I stuck with him, we would do something great.

"While it turned out okay, the first year was devastating. Nothing happened. My peers would ask me what I was doing, and I'd have to say, 'Well, we're looking.' Other people were doing deals, making money, and I was doing nothing.

"But I always knew we would find something, and I really had this belief in what we could do with it. And then we found Commercial Credit, which was kind of . . . well, it was in Baltimore. But it was good enough. It was a platform on which we could build, and we were ready to go. And anyway, it's far more fun to take something like that and make it really good than just inherit something that is already really good."

From this example, it is clear that Dimon has had a strong backbone from early on in his career. He did not have to stay with Weill; job opportunities were available to him. But he was committed to what they could accomplish.

Dimon was so confident of their eventual success that he would rather have failed than abandon the opportunity of giving it a try.

What Dimon was willing to suffer for was, in part, an organization that would work hard to make a difference by doing things the right way and providing a culture that welcomed everyone's opinions.

"I wouldn't have worked at a place where thought was disallowed. If it didn't have some of the values that I cherished, then what would be the point of being there?

"The company had to do the right thing for the right reasons. There had to be an open environment and a different set of values. What mattered was that people could have their own opinions. Because if they couldn't," Dimon asks, "what value would anyone add?"

Again, by Dimon's confession backbone is fueled by the desire to do something right. It is easier to face opposition when one is fighting for something one believes in. What is unique about this example, however, is the direction it takes. Dimon needed backbone to help create a company that did things the right way for the right reasons.

One of the more unjust outcomes of the formation of Citigroup was the dismissal of Dimon a mere month after he orchestrated the merger between Weill's Travelers Group and Citicorp. Recalling the night he found out, Dimon says, "I was having people over for something related to the bank. Sandy [Weill] and John Reed, CEO of Citicorp (parent of Citibank), arrived early to go over the organization and a bunch of issues with me.

"So, here we are, in a room, the two of them sitting across the table from me. That's when they asked for my resignation. What could I do? I said, 'Okay, that's fine.' And that was it. Obviously, they had thought it through, and well, what power did I have to stop them?"

After his dismissal, Dimon spent two years on the sidelines. While he looked at a number of openings, none were in line with his goals. As was the case when he waited with Weill for Commercial Credit, Dimon was willing to suffer the embarrassment of sitting idly before he sacrificed his idea of what he wanted to do next. He waited for the right opportunity to present itself. And while few thought Bank One to be the path that would lead Dimon back to the top of the finance industry, it proved to be yet another platform from which he could do great things.

It is rare to find people who have achieved success, met failure and then accomplished, arguably, an equal or greater success. That is what Jamie Dimon did as he turned Bank One around and orchestrated the merger with J.P. Morgan Chase. He shares his perspective on how he went about accomplishing all of this:

"When people have failed, there's something about them getting back up and going at it again that I respect and admire. But certain questions have to be asked if you're going to persevere and get all the way back or maybe even move forward. In a way it's a type of internal conversation.

"You've got to know if you've learned from your mistakes or if you're destined to repeat them. Because if it's the latter, it seems to me that your fate will always be not to get what you want."

Not that he made many, but Dimon learned from the mistakes he made while working with Weill. From that, he knew, before he even took the Bank One job, what was required to build a great financial institution.

"If you asked me what my goal was[for Bank One], I would have said to build one of the best financial services companies in America. If you asked me what was the chance, if I were being honest I would have told you I would do everything in my power, short of dying or killing to do it, but it was a long shot.

"And now," he says, "With the J.P. Morgan deal, I can legitimately say we want to build the best financial services company in the world. With this platform, it's possible."

Dimon admits that in coming to Bank One, not many people expected him to make the firm a viable candidate to be one of the best in the country, and with J.P. Morgan Chase, one of the best firms in the world. But he reports being open and straightforward about the challenges he saw and what the firm and its employees had to do to overcome them.

"[In] my Chairman's Letters, I talked about what we had to do in very basic terms. One of them is almost exactly what I told the board the second or third time I met them. I don't know if it was strength or foresight or ridiculousness, but when the board started to get interested in me, and I was going for what was likely to be my last interview, I decided that I was going to tell them what I would do, and who I was.

"I took them through what the first 100 days would be like, how I was going to handle people and what I was going to accept and not accept. This was all in very specific terms. I told them, if you don't want me to do that job, don't hire me. This is a marriage. It's hard enough as it is without fighting. That's what I'm going to do. I'm telling you very openly, so that you say this is what we want or what we don't want. I'm fine either way.

"If I had not gotten this job because of that, by being too straightforward or forceful, maybe I'd still be in New York, I'd be working somewhere, but I never would have had all these opportunities. You could have easily said, 'That was stupid, why did you do that?'"

Dimon did it in order to make sure that what he thought was important for the firm's turnaround would not be lost. He believed in doing something right and was not going to back away from that. Dimon's main objective during the interview process was not just to secure the job, but to be given the opportunity to turn this financial institution into something stronger than it had ever been. As a result, he was not willing to water down his responses to what he thought the board wanted to hear, but insisted on providing them with real intelligence on how the company would recover from the financial challenges it faced. To succeed, Dimon had to stand his ground.

Dimon's overview was not easy to hear. He laid out a plan that involved layoffs and cutbacks. But he stood up to the board's challenges and their opposition, knowing that what he was trying to do was right, and that he would eventually succeed—at Bank One or elsewhere. In the end, the board supported Dimon's assessment, seeing that what he was trying to do was well reasoned and in the firm's best interest.

Leadership often means summoning the strength to stand by your convictions even when the stakes are enormously high. When Dimon relates this story, you can see why he has been so successful. It is easy to believe that if you just let him steer the ship, he will guide it safely through danger to a successful outcome.

Contrary to what you might think, Dimon does not view himself as a leader who insists on always doing things his way. "I bend a lot; I am a great compromiser," he says. "The people who work [for me] have to be willing to speak their minds. Often, after someone expresses a frank opinion, I make a point to say, 'God bless you for saying that. I may not agree with everything you said, but I am so glad you said that.'"

But, in the end, what typifies all the leaders in this chapter is that they live by words similar to the ones on which Dimon patterns his life:

"I'm not the type who cares if I fail. I don't care. I care if I don't try. I'll be damned if I don't try."

•   •   •

When trying to determine if someone has backbone, we ask certain questions. What was the riskiest business decision you ever made? Can you make difficult decisions and face the consequences? We ask these questions-because such issues tell us who has the strength to stand by his or her convictions. We want to determine if a person is willing to sacrifice his or her own career and reputation so that something he or she believes in can come to pass. Is that individual willing to stand alone on the proverbial limb?

Can you tell us about a time when you stood by a decision that was not popular? It is easy to approve decisions and support strategies that a large number of people view favorably. It is far harder to back something that is viewed with disdain by others. How people deal with opposition reveals a lot about their backbone. Do they turn their backs on their convictions and succumb to popular opinion or do they redouble their efforts and become even more determined to reach their goals? Leaders with backbone often succeed in changing people's minds with the strength of their convictions. It is exciting to work around someone with backbone. Few people view those with backbone as being just plain lucky or in the right place at the right time.

Can you learn to have a strong backbone? Can you be trained to persevere? Generally speaking, this trait may be hardwired at birth. The degree to which the trait develops certainly is impacted by events in one's life as well as how self-aware an individual may be. A high degree of awareness regarding convictions and values is closely linked to the propensity to stick up for what one believes and is pursuing.

A perspective from the
Russell Reynolds Associates
Executive Assessment Team

A lot of management and leadership research has focused wisely on an individual's abilities in confronting problems and poor performance. Responding to problems efficiently and directly is imperative to a CEO's success. It is also important to stretch this notion of addressing problems further. Executive assessment professionals have found that based on personality data, effective CEOs respond to problems with courage. Effective CEOs also have a tendency to look for problems, searching for and identifying challenges to the organization. Much has been written about the difference between managers and leaders. Leaders scan their environment looking for threats and potential problems before they become serious.

While many CEOs may engage in these "search and rescue" missions consciously for the overall good of their organizations, assessment professionals often find that CEOs are drawn to the adrenaline rush of engaging with problems. While many people naturally prefer to flee a scene involving potential danger, CEOs seem to get a personal "kick" from finding a new problem and fixing it. This, by the way, is why there tend to be two types of CEOs. One type is the emotionally active CEO. Psychologists have noted that emotional people tend to see and identify many problems around them that must be addressed. Therefore, emotionality and passion drive this type of person to be commonly engaged with and immersed in problems. The other type is the principled CEO. This type of person has a bedrock solid set of personal values and beliefs that help them weather storms, ambiguity, and challenges. Therefore, these individuals often end up wading into difficult situations. They endure and persevere based on their deep, guiding set of beliefs that steady them during turbulence.

sources

1. Selected quote, "Perseverance,"
   http://www.quotationspage.com/quotes/Japanese_Proverb/
   (accessed February 20, 2004).
2. Selected quote, "Perseverance,"
   http://www.communicationcenter.com/best_quotes /perseverance.htm
   (accessed February 20, 2004).
3. Laura Colby, "Yank Builds Brit Empire," *Time*, March 23, 1998.
4. Ibid.
5. Selected quote, "Perseverance," http://www.quotegarden.com/failure.html
   accessed March 4, 2004).
6. Ibid.
7. Kentucky Fried Chicken's official website, "Biography Harlan Sanders,"
   http://www.kfc.com/about/colonel.htm (accessed February 15, 2004).
8. Selected history, "Harlan Sanders' Story of Perseverance,"
   http://www.aish.com/literacy/concepts/Perseverance_The_Gateway_to_Holiness.asp
   (accessed February 15, 2004).
9. "Biography Harlan Sanders," http://www.kfc.com /about/colonel.htm
   (accessed February 15, 2004).
10. Milton Hershey School, 'The Milton Hershey Story,"
    http://www.miltonhersheyschool.com/Docs/pubs/miltonhersheystory.htm
    (accessed February 15,2004).
11. Selected quote, "Perseverance," http://www.quotedb.com/quotes/1351
    (accessed February 15, 2004).
12. Kristin Richard, "Time to Get on with Life," April 13, 1998,
    http://www.lancearmstrong.com/lance/online2.nsf/docs/
    FCB9498F568D1DF586256B310009EA24 (accessed February 15, 2004).
13. Sue Shellenbarger, "A CEO Opens up About Loss and Finds He's a
    Stronger Boss," *Wall Street Journal*, September 10, 1997.
14. Selected quote, "Perseverance," http://www.entrepreneurs.com/quotes.html
    (accessed February 15, 2004).
15. Selected quote, "Perseverance," http://www.quotationreference.com/quotefinder.php?
    strt=1&subj=Friedrich+Wilhelm+Nietzsche&byax=1&lr=P(accessed February 15, 2004).
16. Simón Bolívar, "Biography," www.simon-bolivar.org (accessed February 15, 2004; site
    discontinued).
17. Dorothea Lynde Dix, "Biography," http://www.dhhs.state.nc.us/mhddsas/DIX/
    dorothea.html (accessed, February 15, 2004).
18. Selected quote, "Perseverance," http://www.quoteworld.org/browse.php?thetext=persist,
    determination,never%20give%20up&page=2(accessed February 15, 2004).

7

Listening

One of the best ways to persuade others is with your ears—by listening to them.
—Dean Rusk[1]

The way to stay fresh is you never stop traveling, you never stop listening. You never stop asking people what they think.
—Rene McPherson, former chairman, Dana Corporation[2]

WITHOUT THE FACTS, even the smartest person cannot make a good decision. Furthermore, good decisions may not be accepted unless the people affected feel they were given a chance to express their opinions and contribute in some way.

Listening conveys respect for others as it educates and informs the listener of the facts, opinions, and options available. It is an underrated trait that can be a huge asset to a talented leader.

Even the best listeners require a second, complementary skill: knowing when it is time to make a decision and stand by it. There is a time to listen and a time to act.

The willingness to listen, learn and make thoughtful decisions based on the facts is what makes a good leader. Being a great listener goes beyond "hearing." It requires keeping the ego in check and remaining grounded, while shunning the dark sides of pride—conceit and inordinate self-esteem.

No individual has sufficient knowledge, insight, and experience to singularly make all the critical decisions required of today's executive. Put another way, everyone needs help in becoming wise rather than smart. Realizing this need is the first step in developing a willingness to listen and can be the key to your business's growth and survival.

We begin the narrative portion of this chapter with an illustration of how true listening enabled the late Katharine Graham of the Washington Post Company to become one of the most effective leaders of her time. From her example, we hope to illustrate the value that can be gained from this too often ignored but extremely important trait.

●   ●   ●

The facts of Graham's life are known to many; those who are not familiar with her story should take time to read her memoir, *Personal History*, which explains her person and her leadership of the Washington Post Company in great detail. From the very beginning, the success Graham had in running the company was directly derived from her willingness to listen to others.

She came to the Washington Post Company in 1963, thirty years after her father, Eugene Meyer, bought the *Washington Post* newspaper at auction. Her husband, Phil, had recently committed suicide, leaving the company without an executive officer and very much in disarray. Determined not to sell the company that was intimately tied to her life and wanting her children to lead her family's business one day, Graham accepted the board of directors' decision that she become the company's new president. Her genuine feelings for the company and her desire to see it survive drove her to take on the challenge, despite her very limited knowledge of the workings of a newspaper, let alone the diverse media company that the Washington Post Company had become under the stewardship of her husband.

Graham was challenged from the very beginning, forced into situations for which she had no training. While she was insecure in her role as the company's new leader, Graham took it very seriously and made it her mission to learn as much as she possibly could from the men and women (mostly men) who had so dutifully worked for her husband and her father.

The first few years of Graham's tenure as leader were marked by her asking questions and listening to the people who knew the most about the company—specifically the newspaper, with which she was most familiar and comfortable. While Graham realized that she could be a pest and a hindrance to people trying to do their jobs, she was not willing to lead through others.[3]

Graham would not let the hurt egos of others or her own feelings of inferiority stand in the way of doing her job. If she was to meet her obligations, she needed to be as knowledgeable as possible in all aspects of the company's business. Otherwise she would not be equipped to make necessary decisions, failing the very company she so badly wanted to save. Moreover, a leader is only an effective listener and able to secure important information if he or she has the confidence to ask questions, especially those that may sound dumb. After all, the "dumb" questions are often the ones that everyone has. If they are not answered, then questions and doubt remain, rendering the leader less effective.

Over time, Graham became more comfortable with her new life, listening carefully and gaining the trust of those whose advice she sought. She became more equipped to work with and relate to other people, and consequently was better able to handle the overwhelming challenges both the newspaper and the company would face.

Graham was far from the first executive to approach the work environment with questions and she certainly will not be the last. Rose Marie Bravo, now CEO of the British clothier Burberry, was vigilant in asking questions when she was appointed chairman and CEO of the I. Magnin and Bullocks Wilshire department stores in 1989.

Sitting with her store manager and operating vice president, Betty Leonard, Bravo asked questions that might at first have seemed frivolous. She was not concerned with sales figures or inventory turnover. She was more interested in Los Angeles social events. She needed to know who was in attendance and what they were wearing. Were there any special trends, colors or common designers?

Bravo's questions were not without purpose—and nor were Katharine Graham's. The nature of their respective industries demanded that they ask their questions. Knowing what people were wearing to Los Angeles social events informed Bravo of what was being purchased from I. Magnin's Beverly Hills store. And since this location was the barometer for all other stores in the chain—half of the company's business was done in Southern California and Arizona—Bravo's questions made her better aware of the items that would drive the company's growth for that season.[4] Similarly, Graham's questions better informed her of the drivers of the Washington Post Company's growth.

•　　•　　•

Graham's willingness to listen was essential to her becoming more comfortable in her unexpected role. But more than that, listening enabled Graham to improve the paper, both in its layout and in the way journalists and readers viewed it.

It is important, we think, to note that Graham's effectiveness as leader goes well beyond the role she and the *Washington Post* played during the Watergate era. To that end we cite two other examples of how she used her listening skills both to better herself as a business leader and to improve her company.

The first has to do with changes made at the *Post* after the arrival of the new managing editor, Ben Bradlee, in 1965. Many people at the paper had long been tired of the section "For and About Women." Bradlee proposed the creation of a new section and, with the help of his editorial team, outlined a piece that focused on "people, rather than events and on private lives rather than public affairs."[5] Moreover, the new section was not gender specific, but of interest to Washingtonians of "both sexes, black and white, suburbanite and city dweller, decision-maker and home-maker."[6] It would be called "Style."

When it first appeared in the paper, Graham was uncomfortable with the direction of the new section. She confronted Bradlee repeatedly with her concerns. Bradlee's response, which gives one insight into his relationship with his boss, is interesting, as is the final outcome. Recalling the incident, Graham wrote in her memoir:

> Once he cautioned me: "Give us time. It's coming." Another time he said to me sharply, "Get your finger out of my eye"—a stern directive that shook me up, especially because he had always been so good tempered. It upset me enough so that I was able to cool down; I realized I had

pushed too hard. I had improved, but I still tended only to see what was wrong and to ignore what was right.[7]

Graham was well aware of her tendency to be too direct in her criticism. But what is most valuable in this recollection is the tone taken by Bradlee. Here, Bradlee all but admonishes his boss. While such candor is not appropriate to all situations, in this instance, it underlines Bradlee's comfort with Graham, and his understanding that she would listen to him. And as the last sentence of the excerpt indicates, Graham did listen. Despite the misgivings she had with the "Style" section, Graham took Bradlee's advice and left it alone.

Under Bradlee's directorship, the paper broke out of its mold and embraced what was becoming important to its readership. Women's and men's issues were beginning to come together, and neither one wanted to keep on reading about "women holding teacups around a table."[8]

Over time, Graham's decision to listen to Bradlee was validated as the section turned into all that Bradlee envisioned. It became interesting, and soon newspapers all over the country were copying its format.

When we think of the strongest leaders, we know that their strength lies in the ability not to act when all indicators call for them to do so. The decision of whether to act is made exponentially easier when all the facts of the situation are known; and few ways are better than listening when trying to secure knowledge.

The second example that highlights how important listening was to Katharine Graham's career involves her decision to publish the Pentagon Papers in 1971. The verdict was made over the phone, on June 17, 1971. The answer from Graham to outside counsel, Frederick Beebe, was simply, "Go ahead, go ahead, go ahead. Let's go. Let's publish."[9]

The Pentagon Papers were articles commissioned in 1967 by Robert McNamara, then the U.S. Secretary of Defense. Their subject was the decision-making process that led to the United States' initial entry into Vietnam and ultimately to the conflict. McNamara thought they would serve future researchers as "raw material from which they could re-examine the events of the time."[10] They were secret until the *New York Times* baited its readers by mentioning them in a story on June 13, 1971. The *Times* followed up the next day with its first news stories relating to the previously hidden documents.

On June 15, the *Times* was asked by the U.S. government to suspend all future publication of all stories relating to the documents. The *Times* respectfully declined to honor the government's request. The government, in turn, asked for and received a court injunction, stopping the *Times* from publishing anything further on the subject.

The *Post* received its own copy of the Pentagon Papers—which was necessary if it was to write anything original on the subject—on June 16. While the injunction against the *Times* did not apply to the *Post*, Graham was faced with her own specific set of challenges.

First, if the paper published anything related to the Pentagon Papers, it would open itself up to severe criticism; people could view it as defying the law. Second, if the Washington Post Company was involved in a criminal activity, then the underwriter of its pending IPO—Lazard Freres—would be free to terminate its contract. Third and finally, if the *Post* published articles related to the Pentagon Papers, it could open itself up to prosecution under the Espionage Act. If the government could argue successfully that the paper was in violation of this law, the Washington Post Company would be designated a felon, resulting in the loss of its valuable television stations.[11]

Before making her decision, Graham listened carefully to the reasons not to publish—most of which came from the company's lawyers. But she also listened to her reporters and editorial staff, who were in support of publishing articles related to the papers. If Graham decided not to publish, they said, the *Post* would be publicly accused of cowardice; many people would think it gutless and the paper would lose its credibility. An implicit consequence was that most of the paper's best reporters would also leave.

In this decision, Graham knew, was the future of the newspaper. Deciding to publish could be its ruin, but then so too could not publishing. Before saying anything, Graham thought carefully about what she had heard from each side, making sure that all of the big issues were out in the open and that she understood everything.

In the end, Graham's decision was based on the possible outcomes. There is a difference between certainty and uncertainty, and her decision, to which she could have come only as a result of listening, was in keeping with that difference. The *Post*'s first independent story relating to the Pentagon Papers appeared on June 18.

The decision to publish articles about the Pentagon Papers was a seminal one in the history of the *Washington Post*, because suddenly the paper was viewed as being the equal of the *New York Times*. This long-term goal of both Graham and Bradlee was made possible by the paper's decision to stand its ground and speak strongly for the liberties of the press.

Throughout her tenure as leader of the Washington Post Company, Katharine Graham listened to those around her. She never made a blind decision. She was successful because she did not come to conclusions until after all the arguments were made. By taking such measures, she guaranteed that the Washington Post Company would take the right road.

● ● ●

Cameras follow *New York Times* reporter Thomas Friedman when he films a TV special. He moves back and forth between conversations with Israelis and Palestinians, talking to people who are separated by ideology, history, violence, fear and religion.

Watching Friedman, viewers witness how good he is at actively listening to what people have to say. He looks them in the eye and concentrates on what they say. His head nods constantly, conveying understanding and respect. He asks numerous questions and works hard to clarify how they feel. It does not matter that thirty minutes ago he may have been granting equal respect to someone the current speaker might consider his or her mortal enemy; people like talking to Friedman.

Creating a sense of inclusion and knowing that people want to be heard is an important element to listening. Respected by Graham and Friedman, it

---

Mastering the art of listening

Have no preconceived notions. By that I mean don't make any assumptions about what the other party is thinking. Right or wrong, your assumptions will keep you from hearing what's being said. . . .

Always assume that everyone else in the room is smarter than you are. If you get the idea you can outsmart other people, you stop paying attention to them. So I bring a yellow pad with me. On the fourth or fifth page, I write the word "dummy" three times. Whenever I catch myself thinking how brilliant I am, I open the pad to that page, give myself a silent whack, and go back to listening.

—Norm Brodsky, entrepreneur and columnist for *Inc.* magazine[12]

---

is not lost on others, either especially William Wrigley Jr., CEO of the Wm. Wrigley Jr. Company.

Taking over a company his namesake founded in 1891 and led at one time by both his father and grandfather, when appointed to his role in 1999 Wrigley was in the position not to listen to anyone. And while he admits that he tries not to manage by consensus, he knows and readily accepts the benefits he gains from listening to others. His confidence in making a decision and of being a leader comes after he has heard from the people he depends on and trusts.

Wrigley's view of leadership is an expansive one. For him, being a leader is about taking care of a company's culture and system of values. When he speaks of what is gained by listening, he makes reference to things that may appear to be "soft" to many of us. However, the strong leader pays as much attention to the "soft" issues as he or she does to the "hard." A company's success is as much a result of the feelings people have toward the place they work as it is from any corporate decision to pursue an acquisition.

In his own words: William Wrigley Jr.

"I SPEND A LOT of time getting input from and listening to people. This is absolutely an environment where you are free to challenge, question and probe what's going on in the company and what it should be doing. . . . I used to be much more sensitive to our strategy and what we were going to do, but what I've come to realize is that success really lies more in the ability to execute against that strategy, and execution depends, in large part, on living the values of the company."

Because he feels that the key driver to the Wm. Wrigley Jr. Company is its people, Wrigley spends a lot of his time focusing on company values and corporate culture. Explaining his motivations, Wrigley says, "Sure, I have input on marketing and strategy and so on, but at the end of the day, if we don't have the right culture, we're not going to be able to execute our strategy effectively."

While Wrigley is willing to make a hard decision, he tries to limit the number of decisions he makes, so as to better empower others. "I try to stay close to significant people, organizational or cultural issues, which are likely to have a cultural impact on the company, or to make a statement about who we are and what our values are. I'll listen to management and employees, and

I'll try to weigh in—or, if need be, make the call—on that sort of thing. That's really protecting the soul of the company.

"Obviously, when it comes to acquisitions I make the final call, but I base that a lot on how comfortable the management team feels, because even if I feel confident, if the management team doesn't, then we are not going to get very far.

"In many cases, we discuss the different issues. And if we achieve consensus, that's fine. But at the end of the day, people know that's not what we have to do, because I don't want to compromise us down to the lowest common denominator."

So often the results of the group decision-making process are watered-down solutions, supported by the majority but seldom effective once implemented. It is a trap that many leaders fall into, and it is one that Wrigley, when he speaks of avoiding the lowest common denominator, is trying hard to avoid. Too often, when listening, leaders relieve themselves of their responsibilities as final arbiter of what is good for the company; they do not act decisively. Instead, their decisions are an amalgamation of many people's opinions. Listening is effective when it helps a leader come to a better decision; it should never be used as an alternative to better judgment.

> Of all the skills of leadership, listening is one of the most valuable—and one of the least understood. Most captains of industry listen only sometimes, and they remain ordinary leaders. But a few, the great ones, never stop listening. They are hear-aholics, ever alert, bending their ears while they work and while they play, while they eat and while they sleep. They listen to advisers, to customers, to inner voices, to enemies, to the wind. That's how they get word before anyone else of unseen problems and opportunities.
>
> —*Fortune*, April 1994[13]

In addition to listening to the advice of his management team, Wrigley listens to the entire workforce as it relates to improving the company's culture and value system. The Wm. Wrigley Jr. Company conducts cultural surveys, which give the firm's leadership a stronger sense of how employees feel. Questionnaires are distributed to all 13,000 employees. The response rate for the most recent survey was 92 percent, up slightly from the previous study.

Says Wrigley, "That tells me that people wanted to respond, because they felt like they were listened to the first time, as opposed to saying this is just another management sham. We were really encouraged by that; we translated it into fourteen different languages."

The survey is a far-reaching attempt to gather a whole host of information, ranging from how employees feel about the company, its values, principles, and strategy, to the way they perceive compensation, benefits, communication, measured risk, and leadership.

"We take that information," says Wrigley, "and slice and dice it on a cross-functional, functional, regional, geographic, and location-specific basis. Then we create action plans out of it to address issues that are out there."

●　　　●　　　●

When we think of listening it is important to take note of who is being listened to. Different constituencies will provide a leader with different types of information. A person's ability to grasp the big picture is thus dependent on his or her willingness to take information from those who are not only close to him or her, but also from those far removed. In simpler terms, it is as important to listen to customers as it is to your team and workforce. In fact, the most valuable listening often takes place at the customer level.

Paul Tagliabue, commissioner of the National Football League (NFL), knows this, believing the most important part of his job is to pay attention to the fans. He says, "In the context of a sports league, owners have certain interests and so do players. And these interests most often come to clash in collective bargaining negotiations. The media, too, has a perspective, which is sometimes self-interested, but nevertheless, it's there and must be recognized. The fans, who are the customers in this context, I think, are the most disinterested. They can take it or leave it. They can choose one sport over

> Once you have surrounded yourself with good people, listen to them. . . .
>
> Talented people don't want you to come to them and say, "Here's what I'm going to do. What do you think?" They want you to set up issues in terms of, "Here are the challenges we face. What do you think?" If you harness their intellect this way to help solve a problem, they will reach out and help you. Once you've surrounded yourself with good people and are investing in them, you need to listen and respond to them, even when they give you answers you'd rather not hear.
>
> —Joseph Neubauer, chairman and CEO of ARAMARK Corporation[14]

another. Therefore, they are the most important; they are the barometer of how well we're doing and what we should be doing."

Few business leaders listen and have listened to their customers as intensely as Avon's chairman and CEO, Andrea Jung. Arriving at Avon in 1994, Jung was tasked to create a global brand. At the time, each region was in charge of its own campaigns. As a result, the image a South American consumer had of the company was far different than the one held by a North American. Everything, from the logo to the packaging to the advertisements, was different.

While she trusted her own instincts, Jung realized that it was essential for her to get customer input to meet the requirements of her job effectively. She listened to research and customer demographics, both telling her that while the largely middle-class customer base of Avon could not afford Lancôme or Estée Lauder, they still sought the panache and style associated with those more expensive brands. Reacting, Jung redesigned Avon's packaging. The makeup bottles and jars were made more modern and sophisticated, appearing as if they were from upscale department stores.[15]

Further opening herself to customer expectations and desires, Jung became an Avon Lady. Recalling the experience, Jung said in 2001 that she wanted to go through the selling experience by going door to door. Only by doing that was she better able to understand the big issues facing the company. Customers told her of their frustration over colors being discontinued, orders being mismanaged and promotions being confusing. With this information in hand, she was better able to form the brand's identity.

Becoming CEO in 1999, Jung used what she had learned from the company's customers to create Avon's turnaround plan. Developing blockbuster products and selling Avon in retail stores—something that had never been done in the company's history—became the new foundation for growth. The investment community was critical at first, but as time has passed Jung's assessments have proven to be spot on.[16]

While listening to customers can provide a leader with intimate insight into what might be wrong with a product offering, taking the advice of their advisors and management team offers an executive a fix on the current business landscape and what is on the horizon.

In our examination of Katharine Graham's career at the Washington Post Company, we have seen evidence of how listening helps resolve current problems. Paul Tagliabue offers proof of how important the trait is when being confronted by an unknown future. Says Tagliabue:

"We worry a lot about the future health of [football]. [The NFL] has been very good at keeping aware of what affects us at the highest level. But when looking at what was affecting college football and what was affecting youth football, we found out that there was a lot that we didn't know. And that's dangerous because our future depends on future players and the continual interest of the fans.

"We started to ask questions. But it wasn't easy because we didn't know who we needed to listen to. We discovered that parents, school principals, high school coaches and youth football coaches had issues.

"So we reached out and started to invite high school coaches to meetings and asked them if they were facing any problems and what those were. If there weren't any, we wanted to know why. In addition, we conducted research among parents and kids to determine what they wanted out of youth sports.

"We found that kids wanted an active social experience in which they could learn the game and have fun. Parents wanted safe and socially constructive programs that promoted values, education and family. They also sought coaches who were well trained and supportive. We listened and these became the tenets that the NFL's Play Football programs are founded on."

According to Tagliabue, if the NFL was going to maintain its status as the number-one spectator sport in America, and if fans were going to continue to come to stadiums in the future, then a new type of youth football had to be developed, one tailored to the interests and needs of both children and their parents.

"It was born out of listening to what people wanted," Tagliabue says. "The Play Football programs teach self-esteem, discipline, and goal-setting skills. Also, they emphasize safety, fun and teamwork. Coaches are trained to support these goals, and I think everyone involved is optimistic about future results."

Because Tagliabue believes the NFL to be the official caretaker of football, he says he will continue to listen to the concerns of others and look for new ways for future generations to be involved in the game.

"Something we've been thinking about is trying to get one thousand additional doctors from around the country to commit to being team physicians," he says. "One of the big problems in all high school sports, but particularly football, is medical supervision or lack thereof. So one big measure of success might be to double the number of physicians. I think parents would be more comfortable letting their kids play, and kids, I hope, would play longer as a result."

By taking the counsel of others, Tagliabue is prepared for meeting future needs and is now better able to protect and support both the game of football and its players. Thus, in addition to creating a sense of inclusion, listening remains one of the best tools to find solutions to both current and potential challenges.

•　　•　　•

Listening contains a subtle but powerful element. So often a leader listens to gather facts or become better informed of the big picture. We take for granted that this can only happen when others present information—or what they know. This, however, is not true. Another way listening can help a leader gain a sense of the big picture is to pay attention to what is not being said. Bill Gates elaborates on this notion in his book *Business @ the Speed of Thought: Succeeding in the Digital Economy*:

> I like good news as much as the next person, but it also puts me in a skeptical frame of mind. I wonder what bad news I'm not hearing. When somebody sends me an e-mail about an account we've won, I always think, there are a lot of accounts nobody has sent mail about. Does that mean we lost all of those? This reaction may seem unwarranted, but I've found there's a psychological impulse in people to send good news when bad news is brewing. . . .
>
> You have to be consistently receptive to bad news, and then you have to act on it. Sometimes I think my most important job as CEO is to listen for bad news. If you don't act on it, your people will eventually stop bringing bad news to your attention. And that's the beginning of the end.[17]

Gates uses what he is not hearing as a way of getting a better understanding of the situations and environments in which Microsoft competes. Being an effective listener has a lot to do with being perceptive and being able to read between the lines. It is natural for people to avoid discussing what is wrong, particularly when they suspect they may be blamed for the failure or missed opportunity. Yet, that information could be the most crucial information a leader needs to know. Therefore, leaders must be sensitive to what they are not hearing and seek the information as well as demonstrate a desire to hear bad news.

•   •   •

Listening can become increasingly difficult as an individual achieves more success. The higher one advances within the organization, the more the number of demands and distractions increases disproportionately. Also, successful individuals know what has worked for them in the past to make them successful, causing, albeit subconsciously, a built-in resistance to learning new techniques. Learning to listen can be particularly difficult for those whose star rose based on the ability to make hard decisions and "grind" it out. It is tempting to dismiss various opinions based on age, experience, conversation style, or merely the fact that one's mind has already been made up.

> In a talk to the Drucker Foundation Advisory Board in 1993, Peter Drucker said, "The leader of the past was a person who knew how to tell. The leader of the future will be a person who knows how to ask."[18]

But the more one gives in to these temptations, the greater their disadvantage and the greater the likelihood of being blindsided by a major problem they never saw coming.

Jeroen van der Veer, president of Royal Dutch Petroleum Company and vice chairman of Royal Dutch/Shell Group, observes, "If, as a leader, you learn to adapt your thoughts to the facts, then as a leader you will be more sustainable." He adds, "Entrepreneurs listen, think, and do something. We need to reflect, which is in-depth listening."[19]

One way to overcome the tendency not to listen carefully is to be reminded just how much careful listening can accomplish. Nandan Nilekani, CEO of Infosys, the global software company, pointed out to us that because he is a generous listener his customers are more likely to open up to him and share valuable information. "And that's worked very well for me," he says.

Obviously, by listening, someone can acquire more information, in greater detail. But the person can also discover and understand previously hidden biases and capabilities the speaker possesses—or lacks. In this way, a business leader learns why certain projects struggle and others succeed.

On some occasions, by listening carefully, the person speaking is able to solve his or her own problem. If the listener asks superficial questions—or does not listen to replies—he or she will likely be rewarded with superficial answers. But by probing and encouraging the information deliverer to give a detailed, in-depth response, the listener can help the speaker think more carefully and with more focus.

Although we say more developed listening skills are rarer than some of the other leadership traits we are discussing, the basics of how to listen are fairly simple. But how often are the simplest things the most difficult to adapt?

Dave Pottruck, CEO of the Charles Schwab Corporation, has worked incredibly hard at learning to listen actively and at recognizing the degree to which his sheer size, presence, and lofty position can intimidate others. He describes what happened earlier in his career when a superior gave him a review that opened his eyes for the first time to how others perceived him.

In his own words: Dave Pottruck

"I'M AN INCREDIBLY hard worker," says Pottruck. "In my mind, I'm doing it the right way. I'm not backstabbing people . . . I'm not taking credit for other people's work. . . . I'm just working really hard, doing really well and moving up the career ladder.

"What I didn't understand was that everyone around me resented me— for many reasons. They resented me because for one reason or another they couldn't work as hard as I did . . . it was sort of a standard that they didn't want to live up to.

"But, beyond that, there was a self-indulgence and an arrogance in my attitude about myself and my colleagues. I didn't invite other people into what I was working on. You were either on my team—meaning you reported to me—or you were not on my team. My peers were not my partners. They were merely other people who worked for the company. My behaviors did not invite partnership.

"The big turning point for me was my 1990 performance appraisal delivered by my boss, Larry Stupski, who worked as hard as I did, and who was a lot smarter than I was. His ability to master the facts and contribute was incredible to me, so I admired and deeply respected him."

At this point, Pottruck was president of the Charles Schwab brokerage company, which was the largest operating unit of the parent company Charles Schwab Corporation, of which Stupski was the head.

The skill of active listening

The Maryland Leadership Workshops, a nonprofit organization that has been providing comprehensive leadership training to students since 1955, created this concise summary of the skill of active listening, which we have adapted slightly.

1. Avoid distractions, interruptions and interrupting.
   - Allow the speaker to finsh the statement before jumping in to speak, even if you think you know what the person about to say.
   - Use positive nonverbal cues to encourage.
2. Use positive nonverbal cues to encourage.
   - Maintain eye contact with the speaker, even if he or she looks away from you when speaking.
   - Be aware of your facial expressions and body language.
3. Don't fake understanding, ask questions.
   - Example: "Could you give me an example?"
   - Example: "How did you feel when that happened?"
4. Provide clear, unambiguous feedback; paraphrase.
   - Provide acknowledgments (verbal: "I see"; nonverbal: silence, nods).
   - Be specific and descriptive.
   - Stay directed; focus on the speaker's feelings.
   - Be well timed; vary your responses and reflect during brief interactions.
5. Repress the desire to respond with advice or an opinion unless asked to.[20]

"[Stupski] told me that none of my colleagues trusted me because they all believed I had my own agenda. He also said I was too persuasive. I started to argue that being persuasive was supposed to be a strength, when he said, "Dave, a lot of things that are good are great up to a point, and then you reach that point and they're not good anymore. When you don't invite your peers' counsel in the plans, you display a lack of respect for them. It's your plan. You have this incredible sense of ownership, which is good to a point, but you go beyond that point."

Pottruck describes a classic situation with which many confident executives struggle. The talent and energy that brought him into a leadership position became a liability as he rose in the organization. The difference between Pottruck and many other executives is that he was willing to confront these challenges.

Pottruck continues his recounting of this pivotal conversation. "[Stupski] told me that I came in with ideas and showed them, but I didn't invite others to discuss them. I didn't say to others, by listening to them, that I respected and valued their counsel.

"This idea was as foreign to me as saying, 'I want you to go run the Schwab office in Moscow.' Once I invited dialogue, I would lose my ability to control the situation, and everything would just take more time. I had this incredible sense of urgency ticking inside of me that made me rush through everything. And, of course, everybody hated that because we never had important discussions in a calm or supportive environment. I wouldn't let anyone finish a sentence; I was too busy getting on with doing what needed to be done."

At the same time, Pottruck was ending his second marriage, and he readily admits to seeing a therapist who told him that he didn't have the skills to collaborate. Recalls Pottruck, "She showed me that I was listening to figure out my argument, instead of coming to conversations curious to understand the full perspective of the other person. She made me see that when the other person is smart and thoughtful, I could actually end up with a collaborative outcome that's better than anything either of us could do separately. So I started working on these things. And I was flabbergasted. I was astounded by the impact."

Years later, Pottruck reflects on the results of leveraging this different approach. "I've come to the conclusion that I don't know everything. I now respect that I could end up in a different place—make a different decision—than I anticipated after listening to the other people at the table. I try to be collaborative and team-oriented and drive for creative breakthroughs. And I have this notion that I'm trying to inspire commitment, not compliance."

Even today, hearing how Pottruck describes his transformation, one can see that being an active and careful listener is not easy. It takes time and one must be deliberate in one's intentions. Pottruck made the effort because he, like so many others, recognized that listening could make him a better person as well as a better leader. As he changed his style and employed listening and reflection, even though he never lost his energy or drive, people were more willing to work with him. Pottruck's personal life improved as well, which, while not a tale for this book, offers a lesson most will find appealing—listening works as well at home as at the office.

• • •

We begin our summary of this chapter by turning to Henri de Castries, chairman of the Management Board and chief executive officer of AXA.

Having come to AXA from the French Treasury in 1989, de Castries views listening as one of the tools pivotal in his ascent from the company's finance department to its executive suite, where he is now charged with building on the work of Claude Bebear, the "godfather" of the French financial industry. As a result, de Castries is able to show—far better than most—how truly important is the ability to listen, for a leader and a company:

"You learn more by listening than by talking because listening puts you in a receptive mode. Before acting, you need to understand your situation. To maximize your efficiency, you have to start by listening; that is how you are going to learn. And eventually, this attracts opportunities that you would not obtain by yourself. You will benefit from information that has been collected by the people to whom you need to listen."

Like most effective leaders, de Castries knows when to stop listening and make a decision. He explains, "There is a point where you have make a decision, and then make it clear. But I think that to be effective, you have to understand what the alternatives are and how people feel about them, and then make your own choices."

If, on the other hand, warns de Castries, "You do not listen to what people say, then you are missing an opportunity to build consensus and bring everybody on the same boat."

Martin Luther King Jr. stated, "Nothing pains some people more than having to think." [21] Of all the traits we discuss, listening may require the most thinking. Listening means taking in information, reflecting upon and digesting that information, responding to it and integrating it into the task at hand. It takes time, patience, humility, and the art of considering the unlikely. It means considering what is absent as well as what is present, and accepting that the truth may be somewhere in between.

As recruiters, it is important for us to find executives who listen. Too few do and companies suffer as a result. All too often, leaders who do not listen alienate others, since their desire to be in the spotlight is too great to allow for more than one opinion.

Thus, when talking to prospective candidates we earmark those who show a willingness to stop and hear what someone else has to say, who do not interrupt and thoughtfully consider what others think. We also notice those who show a willingness to support other people's ideas over their own. It is the mark of a person who is not in constant need for personal credit and who is more likely to be collaborative, rather than dictatorial, in their leadership approach. These people are listeners. They are the ones who take the time to see the whole picture before making a decision. As a result, the companies that they direct are the ones best positioned in the market and best prepared to handle challenges that may come their way.

A perspective from the Russell Reynolds Associates Executive Assessment Team

The ability to go beyond simply hearing what others have to say—to be able to truly listen to and evaluate information in real time—is a rare and valuable skill. That is, leaders may think that their way of operating has worked for them, and thus may be closed off to ideas and processes suggested by others that are unfamiliar.

This type of inflexibility can be detrimental to an organization's growth and development, particularly in changing markets. To be truly effective in this area, a leader must establish an environment in which individuals throughout the organization feel comfortable and encouraged to share new ideas. To the extent that leaders can seek feedback and input from others, and can identify individuals who are capable of serving as sources in particular areas, they can leverage their network to their benefit.

Being able to listen effectively to the ideas of others is related to an individual's openness to experience. Those who are more intellectually curious and open to the ideas of others tend to have an advantage in thinking flexibly, taking risks, and being able to lead change. This is particularly helpful in entrepreneurial settings and in times of change. Active listening not only leads to novel ideas, but it also facilitates perceptions of true buy-in.

Being able to listen effectively requires more than simply hearing others. Active listeners are able to interpret new information effectively and efficiently. They are able to ask probing follow-up questions to gather more information, and are able to link new information across areas to recognize how it may impact different areas of their business.

Active listeners are able to effectively incorporate new information into action plans and fit it into the big picture. Thus, contrary to some expectations that listening is a waste of time, listening can result in greater efficiency.

sources

1. *The Forbes Book of Business Quotations*, ed. Ted Goodman (New York: Black Dog & Leventhal Publishers, 1997), p. 535.
2. Selected quote, "Listening," http://www.highgain.com/html/listening_quotes_2.html (accessed February 15, 2004).
3. While it can be said that the negative feeling people had toward Graham was because of her gender, she herself never thought of it in those terms. In her eyes, whatever difficulty she encountered was more the result of her ignorance of the business than anything else.
4. Betty Goodwin, "Bravo, the Pacesetter for High-Profile Society," *Los Angeles Times*, September 22, 1989.
5. Katharine Graham, *Personal History* (New York: Vintage Books, 1997), p. 414.
6. Ibid.
7. Ibid.
8. Ibid.
9. Ibid., p. 450.
10. Ibid., p. 444
11. Ibid., p. 448.
12. Norm Brodsky, "I've Got a Secret," *Inc.*, March 1998.
13. Peter Nulty and Patty de Llosa, "The National Business Hall of Fame," *Fortune*, April 4, 1994.
14. Joseph Neubauer, "Five Pillars for Leading the Client-Focused Organization," *Leader to Leader* 30 (Fall 2003).
15. Katrina Brooker, "It Took a Lady to Save Avon," *Fortune*, October 15, 2001.
16. Ibid
17. Bill Gates, *Business @ the Speed of Thought: Succeeding in the Digital Economy* (New York: Warner Books, 2000).
18. Peter A. C. Smith, *Developing the "Adult" Leader*, includes a quote from Peter Drucker (Ontario: Leadership Alliance, 2000). Full text available at http://www.tlainc.com/ldrwhpap.htm (accessed March 8, 2004).
19. Jeroen van der Veer, "View from the Top Series' Remarks," lecture, Stanford University Graduate School of Business, Palo Alto, CA, March 10, 2003, http://www.gsb.stanford.edu/news/headlines/vftt_vanderveer.shtml (accessed February 22, 2004).
20. Maryland Leadership Workshops, "How to Actively Listen," http://www.mlw.org/listening.htm (accessed February 17, 2004).
21. Selected quote, "Martin Luther King Jr.," http://www.angelfire.com/sc/pac/quotesk.html (accessed March 9, 2004).

8

Emotional Intelligence

Man must be arched and buttressed from within,
else the temple will crumble to dust.
—Marcus Aurelius Antoninus[1]

If you wish to succeed in managing and controlling others—
learn to manage and control yourself.
—William J. H. Boetcker[2]

ALTHOUGH THE WORDS USED TO DESCRIBE this trait are fairly recent, the trait itself has existed throughout history.

When we speak of emotional intelligence, we refer to one's understanding and management of emotions and one's understanding of and consideration of other people's feelings.

Leaders who show emotional intelligence are the ones most capable of making improvements, both to themselves and to their operations. They are also more likely to be confident in their decisions. The result is that such leaders inspire the confidence of those they direct.

Emotional intelligence seems to result from both nature and application. Some leaders have the trait naturally, but most find it from practice, after recognizing its importance.

Many recognize Elizabeth I as one of history's greatest monarchs. Her leadership genius was in her understanding and appreciation of the culture she shared with her subjects.

Sixteenth-century Britain viewed women through the lens of the courtly tradition. The feminine ideal was to be a virgin of pale skin, fair hair and willowy figure.[3] In many ways, this paragon mirrored the Catholic Church's view of the Blessed Mary, who stood not only as the mother of Christ but also as divinely capable of interceding on behalf of those who made her the object of their prayers.

Elizabeth understood that a weakness of the newly established Protestantism was the diminished role of the Blessed Virgin. Though revered as the mother of Christ, Mary was no longer seen as a figure worthy of independent worship, creating an emotional void in the lives of many people.

To fill this emptiness, Elizabeth transformed herself into the Virgin Queen, thus marrying the courtly ideal to the religious icon. She satisfied a critical need of her people, and in so doing found a means by which to better secure her position as the true monarch of her country.[4]

●　　●　　●

In 1990, John Mayer, a professor of psychology at the University of New Hampshire, and Peter Salovey, a professor pf psychology at Yale University, defined the type of wisdom leaders like Elizabeth I have displayed. They called it emotional intelligence.[5] Their work inspired a number of popular books on the subject and led to widespread recognition of the importance of this trait.

Mayer states, "Emotional intelligence is the ability to reason with and about emotion, and to use emotions in ways that facilitate thought." He continues, "I describe EI abilities or skills as falling within four areas: first, the capacity to accurately perceive emotions; second, to use emotions to facilitate thought; third, to understand

> "American history suggests not only that emotional intelligence is an indispensable ingredient of political leadership but also that it can be enhanced through sustained effort." Gergen goes on to observe about past American presidents that George Washington had to learn to control his temper, Lincoln to control his moods, and Roosevelt to be more empathetic.
>
> —David Gergen,
> adviser to four American presidents[6]

emotions and their meanings, and fourth, to reflectively manage emotion in ways that promote personal growth."

We borrow heavily from Mayer as we begin our own examination of emotional intelligence. To better serve the reader, however, we will explore this trait from three different perspectives:

+ Behaviors and decisions made as a result of how one understands one's emotions

+ Behaviors and decisions made as a result of empathy and appreciation for the feelings of others

+ Instincts and how emotional intelligence underlies our natural abilities to assess situations and make decisions

As with the other traits covered in this book, it is not essential for a leader to possess emotional intelligence in order to be effective. Some can be completely oblivious to the feelings of the people around them or unaware of their own emotions and how those impact behavior and decision making. In fact, a great deal of executive coaching addresses changing the behaviors that have kept an executive from realizing his or her maximum effectiveness. Through the use of 360-degree feedback tools, many senior executives discover late in life that the behavior they thought key to their success actually interfered with their ability to positively motivate and connect with their people. The behavioral adjustments that are required, while seemingly simple on the surface, are profound because of the emotional challenges. We'll address more of this later.

But many great leaders succeed because they do possess this trait, even when they lack the intelligence, schooling, or advantages others have enjoyed. Some call it street smarts, others refer to it as common sense, while still others deem it simply to be instinct. Regardless of the nomenclature, the behavior acknowledged is the ability to be in touch with what is going on around you, as well as within yourself, and making wise decisions that others want to support. While you might argue that you cannot teach common sense or instincts, the fact remains that it is possible to develop your awareness levels and incorporate that awareness to both your behavior and your decision-making process.

Self-awareness comes in many forms and at any stage of life. Jay Fishman, formerly chairman, president, and CEO of the St. Paul Companies, Inc., and now CEO of St. Paul Travelers says, "Early on in my career, I came to an awareness about myself, something so obvious, yet I know it still eludes many people. Simply put, I'm not the most capable person in the world. There are other people who are just as good or better at things than I am. Knowing what I do well and what I don't do so well is what has enabled me to do better. And I'm sure it has enabled many companies to succeed because leaders who possess this ability have the confidence to give responsibility to others, and that has near endless benefits."

> Real knowledge is to know the extent of one's ignorance.
> —Confucius[7]

In addition to appreciating your strengths and weaknesses, emotional intelligence involves recognizing your values and real motivations; in other words, knowing yourself, or to quote Shakespeare, "To thine own self be true."[8] The late psychologist Abraham Maslow, who wrote extensively on human motivation, elaborated on this more complete notion of emotional intelligence:

> Whereas the average individuals "often have not the slightest idea of what they are, of what they want, of what their own opinions are," self-actualizing individuals have "superior awareness of their own impulses, desires, opinions, and subjective reactions in general."[9]

People with emotional intelligence are better able to see where they fit in the world, to take control of their lives, and to put their feelings in context. While this may not always lead to the desired result, they will have a greater sense of knowing what they want and how to get it. If these goals include leading, inspiring or assisting others, then such self-knowledge makes achieving them easier.

Richard Branson, chairman and CEO of Virgin Group, Ltd., is a man who seeks adventure. The way he runs his business accommodates his love of thrills, from his oft-dangerous publicity stunts to his seemingly whimsical forays into new, sometimes perplexing ventures. Branson is also a man who looks at authority with contempt. Consequently, Virgin stands out as being irreverent, always in contrast to anything that can be referred to as "the

160

The different levels of emotional awareness

In an award-winning paper published in *Human Relations*, Professor Jennifer George included this explanation of how people have different levels of awareness of emotions:

Appreciation of the consequences of moods and emotions varies across individuals. Some people have a rudimentary understanding of how they (and other people) are influenced by feelings and use this knowledge in functional ways.

A leader in a negative mood who decides to delay meeting with his followers to discuss upcoming changes in need of his support until he is feeling better intuitively realizes how his ability to enthusiastically communicate information about the changes and garner his followers' support is influenced by his current feelings. Similarly, a home buyer in a positive mood who sees a house she really likes but forestalls making a final decision until she returns to the house in a couple of days in a different "frame of mind" possesses an understanding of how her appraisal of the house may be colored by her good mood.

On the other hand, some people are oblivious to the effects of feelings. A stereotype of obliviousness to the effects of feelings is the family member who has had a hard day at work, comes home in a bad mood, and proceeds to get into arguments with his or her spouse and children. This family member, however, never realizes how his or her bad mood is contributing to the disagreements and, instead, berates everyone else for their presumed failings, intensifying their own bad mood as well as the disagreements.[10]

Establishment." Virgin is one of the world's most recognized brands, Branson one of the world's richest men, and yet his office is merely an overstuffed chair at one end of his living room. Business executives see him as his children see him, among an assortment of running shoes, Rollerblades, and gym bags.

Richard Branson's life is far from terrible—did we mention he owns an island in the Caribbean? One of the reasons that he has done so well is his understanding of who he is and what he is about. By being emotionally intelligent, Branson discovered the values that are most important to him. His desire to remain true to those values resulted in a company that was founded on them. Because so very little separates the man from his enterprise, Branson has been able to become more involved in and more successful at all aspects of his life.

When we think of the emotional intelligence of leaders, in addition to an understanding of themselves, we also think of their sense of knowing their environment and their awareness of the feelings and emotions of those around them. From this understanding, they make judgments and come to more reasonable conclusions as to how they should behave around other people in order to get the most desired results.

A good example of a leader who displays emotional intelligence by being aware of other people's feelings is Marc Breslawsky, chairman and CEO of Imagistics International, which sells, rents, and services copiers and fax machines made by manufacturers such as Matsushita.

In his own words: Marc Breslawsky

OVERCOMING TEENAGE YEARS during which his parents fretted over his bad grades and his "laziness," Breslawsky rose to become president of Pitney Bowes and later CEO of its spin-off, Imagistics International. At the time he left Pitney Bowes, people thought him crazy to leave a comfortable leadership position to head a business the parent company decided to abandon. His reasoning at the time, he says, was that he thought it was the right opportunity at the right time.

What did Breslawsky see that made him willing to risk his career on a spin-off? Or, more to the point, what did he know about himself and others that made him believe that such a move would be successful?

"Intuitively," he says, "I felt that the upside was far greater than the downside. All that was needed was management discipline, and I knew that my team and I could provide that."

That having been said, Breslawsky was realistic about the hurdles he faced. "It was right after 9/11, which increased the risk factor. The economy was bad, making it more difficult to raise the money we needed if we were going to make the decisions necessary to turn the organization around.

"I think one of the reasons for my confidence came from talking to the people who worked in the division that would be spun off. The first thing my management team and I did was to get a feel for how people were going to react to the things we were thinking about. So we went out and listened to the new company's employee base. We tried to get a better sense of how our ideas would affect them.

"Most of them felt that they had tremendous job security [at Pitney Bowes] because they were part of a large corporation, but the truth is there's no job security in a business unit that is doing poorly, as was the case at this division of Pitney."

Thus Breslawsky's strategy incited in people a greater sense of job insecurity. But he tried hard to remedy this feeling, explaining that while they "knew we would have fewer people as we went forward, those fewer people would be more secure and happier in their jobs, because they would be in an organization that was doing well."

Today, as Breslawsky is quick to point out, the morale of Imagistics is the highest it has been in twenty years. Looking back on the days and months leading up to and just after the spin-off, he believes that part of its success was due to him trusting his instincts. He fully admits that those instincts were the result of talking to people, being aware of their feelings, and addressing those feelings when coming up with the appropriate strategies. Thus the type of knowledge he obtained from others helped him make the decisions that would not only be accepted by all, but would also help the business grow.

Throughout the years, leaders like Breslawsky have benefited from the willingness to see and accept the feelings of those around them. Because people are much more

---

A lesson for a young boy

Leaders with EI instinctively understand when they possess the ability to lead others both credibly and effectively. Terry Pearce, who cowrote a book with Schwab CEO Dave Pottruck, tells a story in this regard about Gandhi:

A woman brought her young son to Gandhi and said, "Would you talk to him? He eats too much sugar." Gandhi asked her to bring him back in two weeks. She brought her son back two weeks later, and Gandhi spoke very eloquently about why the boy should stop eating too much sugar. The mother told Gandhi, "That was very effective. But why did you ask me to bring him back in two weeks?" Gandhi said, "I first had to stop eating sugar myself." He knew that he could not express his argument authentically unless he first went through that change himself.[11]

willing to follow someone whom they believe is aware of and sensitive to his or her own feelings, many leaders have increased their effectiveness by improving their appreciation for how their audience or key constituencies view and feel about the issue at hand.

This level of sensitivity relates to markets as well as employees. Founded in a war-torn Tokyo neighborhood in 1946, the Tokyo Telecommunications Engineering Corporation stood out immediately from other Japanese firms. First, it did not develop products for the government. Instead, it chose to design consumer electronic goods. Second, unlike most Japanese industrial firms, it thought its ultimate survival depended not on the local market but on the world market.

In the postwar years, to succeed on a global scale, the management of Japanese companies had to be aware of and overcome the ill feeling foreign consumers had toward Japan and Japanese goods. Many people at the time viewed Japan with prejudice as result of the role it played the war. In addition, Japan was known for producing only cheap toys and plastic flowers. The belief that the Japanese did not have the necessary skills to build reliable electronic products led many to think that there was no reason to buy such goods from a Japanese firm.

Not wanting their company to fall victim to these preconceived notions of animosity and inferiority, founders Akio Morita and Masaru Ibuka knew that a name change was necessary. The new name needed to attract rather than repel the foreign consumer. With that aim, the two men combined *sonus*, the Latin root for sound, with the English diminutive *sonny*.[12] The resulting Sony Corporation was so successful at breaking the company's association with Japan that years later, when Morita was in New York talking to retailers, few of them had any idea that Sony was a Japanese company.

Engineering brilliance was necessary for Sony's success, but so too was the emotional intelligence displayed by the company's founders. The impetus of Sony's early growth was the two men's understanding of the competitive market environment. Would the company have grown sufficiently if it had entered the world market under its original name? We have no way of knowing, but feel confident that the odds of success would have been much lower had they operated as the Tokyo Telecommunications Engineering Corporation.

In 1936, ten years prior to the founding of Sony, Kiichiro Toyoda was trying to determine a brand name for his company's cars, one that would excite both consumers and employees. To that end, he orchestrated a contest, offering a prize to whoever came up with the best name. Twenty-thousand people entered, and the winning response was "Toyota."

While in English this appears only to be a slight tweaking of the family's name, in Japanese the change is dramatic. The family name Toyoda is written in Chinese characters and means abundant rice field. The brand name Toyota, however, is written in katakana, a phonetic alphabet used in Japan for foreign words. Smooth and contemporary compared with "Toyoda," "Toyota" is written in eight strokes, a number which in Japan means increasing prosperity.[13]

Like Sony's founders, Toyoda named his car company by taking into account the feelings and interpretations of others. Toyoda saw the naming process as a way to accelerate his company's growth. Customers associate all that the word *Toyota* meant with his company's cars; and who would not like a car capable of making us feel both modern and successful? People were attracted to the cars as a result of the name. The fact that the car performed well confirmed the association.

It is nearly impossible to exhaust the examples of business leaders and companies who benefited from being aware of the feelings of others. Products as diverse as baby powder and clear cellophane tape were born of simple consideration. The former was more or less the result of Johnson & Johnson answering a doctor's complaint, while the latter was 3M's response to the dire need for waterproof packaging tape.

Nowadays, of course, the entire advertising and branding business is built upon market research. One might argue that all companies exhibit emotional intelligence merely by responding to their research. But we know this is not the case. Many companies miss the mark after having invested heavily in consumer and market research. Some of that is due to poor quality in products and services. A damaged reputation due to product quality or misconduct on the part of management can drive a company to bankruptcy, turn it into an acquisition target or even run it out of business.

Success—individual, product or organizational—has many moving parts, including the external environment over which we have no control. Luck, be it good or bad, plays an enormous role in success, as does timing. The point is that your chances of leadership success will be greatly enhanced by being aware of others and, most important, respecting that information enough to modify your behavior when necessary.

● ● ●

Can emotional intelligence be learned? In Chapter 7, Dave Pottruck, CEO of The Charles Schwab Company, told us how he was made more aware of the impact his behavior had on others and what he did to change that. He became a stronger leader as a result of listening to both his former boss and his doctor. But he also improved by developing his own emotional intelligence.

Pottruck wanted to be viewed as a better leader at Schwab. As he told us, that would not happen until others saw him in a new light. To be viewed differently, Pottruck began managing his behavior and his quirks. Suddenly, he became a person with whom people could relate. This, in turn, made him a better leader.

Recalling our conversation with him, Pottruck says, "[My doctor] showed me that I was listening to figure out my argument, instead of coming to conversations curious to understand the full perspective of the other person. She made me see that when the other person is smart and thoughtful, I could actually end up with a collaborative outcome that's better than anything either of us could do separately. So I started working on these things. And I was flabbergasted. I was astounded by the impact."

Before this, people were not reacting well to how Pottruck treated them. This limited both his ability to accomplish more and his chances for professional advancement. To fully realize his potential, he needed to make improvements. By doing so, he illustrated emotional intelligence. How? The improvements Pottruck made were a reaction to his understanding of both himself and of others. His awareness of himself told him that he wanted to be seen as an effective leader and thus worthy of advancement. His awareness of others informed him that he was not an effective leader and not worthy of advancement. By managing his quirks he was able to address his personal failures and improve his relationships, better guaranteeing the realization of his goals.

Similarly, when Klaus Kleinfeld, member of the Corporate Executive Committee at Siemens AG, was a young executive he worked hard on his ability to better relate to people.

Born in the north of Germany, he never gave up his northern accent. However, in southern Germany, the northern accent is associated with arrogance. Kleinfeld suffered a hard lesson when he realized people were stereotyping him as arrogant due to his accent.

Recalling the experience to us, Kleinfeld says, "What I learned was is that once you have an image, that sticks with you for quite a while. And you really have to do something to manage it. So I decided that I was not going to work on my accent, because you have to be yourself, but I did work on my ability to relate to people so that they could immediately see beyond the accent to the person I am."

So he now jokes about his accent when hosting meetings, spends much of his time walking around and meeting people and has established an open-door policy designed to tear down physical or otherwise perceived barriers.

Over the last decade or so, many executives have tried to up their game by utilizing the services of executive coaching. The approaches to coaching are as numerous as the number of coaches. The outcomes are as numerous as the number of participants. This is a big business based on enough positive results that the industry of coaching continues to grow. We mention coaching here, as opposed to the array of executive development programs that also improve leadership skills, because we are most concerned in this chapter with changing behavior.

Marshall Goldsmith is one of the most highly acclaimed executive coaches in the business. He believes so strongly in his methodology that he collects no fee until the desired behavioral change has taken place. Without question, he believes that executives can learn more effective behavior, though, because he is no fool, he does limit his coaching to those he believes can and are ready to undertake what can be painful change.

Goldsmith, who also heads up the Russell Reynolds Associates Executive Coaching Panel—an independent group that works with our own Executive Assessment team describes his behavioral coaching in the 2003 book *Profiles in Coaching*, which he edited along with Howard Morgan and Phil Hawkins. On the surface, the process is unfailingly simple:

• Involve the leaders being coached in determining the desired behavior in their leadership roles.

• Involve the leaders being coached in determining key stakeholders.

- Collect feedback.

- Determine key behaviors for change.

- Have the coaching clients respond to key stakeholders.

- Review what has been learned with clients and help them develop an action plan.

- Develop an ongoing follow-up process.

- Review results and start again.[14]

In reality, the process can be enormously difficult, because it is based on the participation of stakeholders and their perceptions of the individual receiving the coaching. In relaying his own evolution as a coach, Goldsmith says:

> In phase one—I believed that my clients would become better because of me. I thought that the coach was the key variable in behavioral change. I was wrong. Since then we have done research with over 86,000 participants on changing leadership behavior. We have learned that the key variable for change is not the coach, teacher or advisor. It is person being coached and their co-workers.
>
> In phase two—I spent most of my time focusing on my coaching clients. This was much better. I slowly learned that a hard-working client was more important than a brilliant coach! I learned that their ongoing efforts meant more than my clever ideas.
>
> In phase three (where I am now)—I spend most of my time not with my coaching client but with the key stakeholders around my client. My results are dramatically better.[15]

What this describes is a highly participative and iterative process where the executive is more vulnerable than perhaps he or she has ever been. It is a risk many are not willing to take; but for those who do, the learning that comes from having a clearer sense of themselves and others takes them to levels of leadership that would have not otherwise been possible.

Mike McGavick, chairman, president and CEO of the insurance company Safeco, has recognized the value of such formal feedback programs, telling us in our interview, "They are rewarding on several levels. As a starting point for executives who want to work on their own potential, the approach enables a person to have a full understanding of who they are. It reveals the good and the bad of how executives are perceived by a number of constituencies.

"The first thing they work on is trying to get you to understand what outcomes certain behaviors lead to. The second thing is creating a detailed plan to address any deficiencies of leadership behaviors. The most important insight that comes out of this process is that the skills and traits that put you in position to be the leader of a company are not the same traits that will allow you to be a successful CEO."

Summing up the program, McGavick describes the ultimate reward as being his definition of emotional intelligence: "You gain this confidence and trust of others, meaning a better understanding of where others are coming from. It involves helping others discover how they can be successful within the company's plans and helping them gain a sense of personal connection, and likely satisfaction, from following through and making the whole organization better."

●　　●　　●

While we believe that it is possible for the willing executive to learn how to increase emotional intelligence by becoming more aware of oneself and others and applying that awareness to behavior and decision making, there remains the third element we mentioned in the beginning of the chapter: instinct. Is it inborn or learned? We now take a closer look.

Robert Johnson is the founder, chairman and CEO of Black Entertainment Television (BET), now a subsidiary of Viacom. His understated, commonsense manner belies significant success; he sold BET to Viacom for $3 billion in a deal that made Johnson Viacom's second-largest individual shareowner after Viacom chairman and CEO Sumner Redstone. Johnson places great importance on his instincts—and by extension his emotional intelligence—saying he enters into partnerships as a result of what his "gut" tells him.

In his own words: Robert Johnson

IN BUSINESS, THE question Johnson first asks himself is whether he wants to be in business with the person on the other side of the table. His or her self-awareness, strengths and weaknesses, and likes and dislikes notify him at the earliest moment whether a deal or partnership is going to be a success.

"Early on in the course of a deal, I make a gut judgment whether I like the person. One of the great advantages to being successful in business is that you can pick with whom you want to do business. Naturally, most people want to do business with someone they like and who can add value. I'm no different.

"When I meet someone, I instinctively know if I like the person, if we have the same values and if this is someone with whom I'd like to have dinner and talk about things other than business. If the answer is yes, then my gut tells me to do the deal."

Johnson admits that having access to money enables him to focus on things that interest him, and people with whom he wants to work. In so doing, he also points out how important emotional intelligence is to his day-to-day business activities.

"When I saw that Hilton wanted to sell hotels, because they had acquired other hotels and needed to diversify some of the assets, I thought, 'The hotel business, I understand it, I'm on the board, it has somewhat of an entertainment feel to it, which is what I am both good at and like.'

"I didn't want to run the hotel acquisition company, so I hired a senior executive from Hilton with whom I could work and who would drive value. That is what I'm passionate about: creating business opportunities and putting people in place to make them work."

Johnson seeks a sense of the big picture from his people. He then weighs his different options against his innate sense of comfort and with what is most important to him. He trusts the people around him to get the details right. But in the end, those details play only a part in the decisions he makes. The fundamentals of each deal must first align with his instincts.

Most of the decisions that Johnson says are based on what his gut tells him which is derived from the work he has already put in to determine what he is good at, what he likes and what is important to him. Knowing these things makes him more comfortable deciding whether to enter into a partnership agreement, as he is made more sure of the alliance's eventual success. You may ask, where does instinct end and analysis and good judgment kick in?

The answer is that the two are not mutually exclusive. Instinct is not used in a vacuum. It could be that instinct is the effective balance between the emotional and the analytical—the left and right sides of our brains.

In Johnson's case, his well-developed emotional intelligence will continue to influence his business decisions. At the close of our conversation, he admitted that he purchased the National Basketball Association's new Charlotte franchise because he wanted to maintain a highly visible role not only for "psychic satisfaction," but also because "it gives me a visible perch that results in other business opportunities." His purchase of the team then was the result of how he saw himself, what his priorities were and what he was comfortable doing—a defining example of a business leader using emotional intelligence to advance his cause.

•   •   •

Every human has instincts. Ancient humans relied almost completely on instinct. Think of our most primitive forebears. The input they used to make decisions came almost exclusively from their senses—sight, smell, hearing, touch, taste—and, of course, experience. One can argue that at present instincts may have been overridden by the incredible access we have to information and the filters provided by cultural biases and prejudices. Has this enormous availability of information combined with an educational bias toward thinking rather than feeling caused us to evolve to a point that we no longer know how to use our natural instincts, particularly in the business environment? Certainly, few executives go before their boards of directors with a business proposition and say, "I just feel this is the right thing to do."

We address the importance of valuing cultural differences in the next chapter. But to conclude this chapter, we want to emphasize how important we feel emotional intelligence—instinct, common sense, street smarts, or empathy—is to being a successful leader in today's business environment.

Leaders lead and managers execute. They are two different, though related, roles. Managing may indeed require specific, learned knowledge, and discreet skill sets. This is not to say that a leader need not have knowledge or skills; indeed, most leaders come into a position to lead because they have displayed above-average skills and sensibilities. What separates those who have leadership capabilities from those who are just good managers may be emotional intelligence, the awareness of how their behavior impacts others and the ability to act effectively on that awareness. This is not a function of education, upbringing, or having advantages. It is at the core of the individual and is about how that person engages with the world around him or her.

Because we believe every individual has instincts, we believe that every executive has the ability to hone his or her emotional intelligence. The desire to do so, the willingness to receive input, and the commitment to modify one's behavior are what distinguish those who will become effective leaders from those who will not.

How then do you recognize your emotional intelligence and that of others? When we are interviewing people for leadership positions, we look for a number of things:

- A track record of growth in management/leadership style, as evidenced by how someone exhibits empathy and the ability to continue to learn from others, always integrating new approaches and demonstrating self-improvement.

- Interest in the world around them, not just their immediate business environment.

- Expressing their views and recounting their experiences in the plural (e.g., we, us, our) versus the singular (I, me, mine).

- Willingness to take on conflict and situations where polarized points of view exist, since reaching effective consensus requires a great deal of empathy.

- Demonstration of strong interpersonal skills, directly and indirectly through the referencing process, remembering how important the "stakeholder" is in validating an individual's leadership style.

A perspective from the Russell Reynolds Associates Executive Assessment Team

As people reach upper levels of an organization and are further along in their careers, they can fall into the trap of confusing expertise with omniscience.

In the initial stages of one's career, it is critical to develop skills and technical expertise. As executives progress, they develop a greater knowledge base and more situational experience. They become savvier in dealing with people and with trends in their businesses. Due to the level of ambiguity and dynamic nature of executive positions, the technical expertise developed early in a career becomes less important in upper-level positions, and richness of experience becomes more important.

As intuition or gut feelings get stronger, people tend to underestimate the value of such feelings, especially considering the amount of experience that leads to strong intuitions. It is important to value data and to pay attention to the advice of others, but decisions are, and should be, made by leaders. That is, leaders must evaluate all forms of input including hard data and the opinions of well-informed colleagues, as well as what their own experiences have taught them.

Successful leaders have the confidence and boldness to make "tough calls" in the face of opposition, when they feel strongly that their decisions are appropriate. Such confidence and risk taking can lead to great success. This often is the dividing point between those who achieve great success thanks to following their instincts and those who ignore gut feelings and make conservative choices that yield little in the way of outcomes. For example, in the 1920s, Walt Disney disregarded the criticism of his colleagues who asserted that the public would not be interested in watching movie-length cartoons, and released the animated film *Snow White*, which was extraordinarily successful and began the popularity of this media form.

sources

1. *The Forbes Book of Business Quotations*, ed. Ted Goodman (New York: Black Dog & Leventhal Publishers, 1997), p. 746.
2. Ibid., 747.
3. Alan Axelrod, *Profiles in Leadership*, (New York: Prentice Hall Press, 2003), p. 158.
4. Ibid., 159.
5. Peter Salovey and John D. Mayer, "Emotional Intelligence," *Imagination, Cognition, and Personality*, 9 (1990): 185–211.
6. David Gergen, "Voices: Leading by Feel," *Harvard Business Review*, January 2004.
7. Selected quote, "Intelligence," http://www.vibrantuniverse.com/knowledge.html (accessed February 22, 2004).
8. William Shakespeare, *Hamlet* (New York: Washington Square Press, 2003) 1.3.55–81. References are to act, scene, and line.
9. Abraham Maslow, *"Motivation and Personality,"* 3rd ed. (Boston: Addison-Wesley Publishing Co., 1987)
10. Jennifer George, "Emotions and Leadership: The role of emotional intelligence," *Human Relations* 53, no. 18 (August 2000): 1027.
11. Terry Pearce, interview by staff of Knowledge@Wharton, June 7, 2000.
12. Brent Schlender, "Sony on the Brink," *Fortune*, June 12, 1995.
13. Bernstein, "Toyoda Automatic Looms and Toyota Automobiles," in *Creating Modern Capitalism: How Entrepreneurs Companies, and Countries Triumphed in Three Industrial Revolutions*, ed. Thomas K. McCraw (Cambridge, MA: Harvard University Press, 1 997), p. 409
14. Howard Morgan, Phil Harkins and Marshall Goldsmith, eds., *Profiles in Coaching* (Burlington, MA: Linkage Incorporated, 2003). Text available at http://www.marshall goldsmith.com/html/articles/changing.html (accessed March 8, 2004).
15. Ibid.

9

Diversity

"I have a dream that my four little children will one day live in a nation where they will not be judged by the color of their skin but by the content of their character."

—Martin Luther King Jr.[1]

What sets worlds in motion is the interplay of differences, their attractions and repulsions; life is plurality, death is uniformity.

Octavio Paz[2]

DIVERSITY IS NECESSARY TO SURVIVE in a complex world. Systems that are diverse are more resilient, and are better able to withstand the challenges presented by an ever-changing and dynamic environment.

In leadership terms, the trait we label as diversity means the ability to bring together people with unique opinions, talents, backgrounds, and heritages and create an organization that is stronger and more successful as a result of these differences.

To be clear, the focus of this chapter goes beyond the formal "diversity programs" that ensure racial or gender diversity within corporations. Rather, we are talking about the leadership trait of actively seeking out and leveraging diverse capabilities and perspectives.

Nature above all teaches us that diversity produces the healthiest ecosystems. Yet humankind's natural inclination is to group around likenesses or similarities—like-minded, like-acting, like-looking people cluster more naturally. Granted, homogeneity has proven to be a survival tactic in and of itself. Throughout civilization, leveraging similarities has brought cohesiveness to communities and organizations and, yes, generals and politicians have used it as a reason to wage war.

However, inbreeding—lack of diversity in the gene pool—can also weaken a species and even render it extinct. In a world as interconnected as ours is in these early years of the twenty-first century, the modern organization needs diversity in order to survive. While "diversity" certainly encompasses specific legislated categories (based on race, religion, gender, sexual preference, and so forth), we also include diversity of thought, opinion, cultural perspective, and approach as types of diversity modern leaders need to incorporate into their style and their teams.

The world is endlessly multifaceted. No leader, however open-minded or worldly, can grasp all the nuances of operating on such a variety of stages. That is why embracing and cultivating diversity is a powerful tool not only for achieving success, but also for prolonging it.

Without diversity in the workplace, leaders would be unable to capably captain businesses through the often volatile and unpredictable waters of multimarket commerce. Because they are often restricted by their own cultural perspectives, these leaders seldom know the appropriate way to act in unfamiliar markets.

Diversity also offers leaders new and alternative perpsectives, which reduces the possibility of leaders being blind to anything that is not right in front of them. Tunnel vision may be eliminated by opening oneself up to various points of view.. Leaders are more informed of what exists on the horizon and are better prepared to handle surprises and challenges as they are neither surrounded by "yes" men and women nor by those whose take on a situation mirrors their own.

In the remaining pages, we will address what a more diverse corporate environment accomplishes and why the desire and willingness to surround oneself with differing opinions is such an important trait for a leader to have. We will also offer ways one can create a more diverse environment, going well beyond the notion of hiring people who have complementary skills but different sensitivities and backgrounds.

* * *

Most organizations make "cultural fit" a key specification when recruiting into the organization. Some interpret this to mean "just like us." In fact, cultural fit is—or should be—more about values than behavior or perspective. This nuance is perhaps the most difficult of all recruiting challenges.

Klaus Kleinfeld, member of the Corporate Executive Committee at Siemens AG, understands this better than most, going so far to say that diversity is both a vital partner to and promoter of any organization's system of values.

In his own words: Klaus Kleinfeld

"THE LEADERSHIP PRINCIPLES for a multicultural environment are no different than leadership principles in a nonmulticultural environment," Kleinfeld says. "Cultural differences probably only come into play about a third of the time.

"Most important are your core principles, which address much deeper elements of the human condition. Every human has a lot of things in common. For example, if you don't show respect for an individual—whether he's Chinese, German, French, or American, you will get a very strong reaction.

"But sometimes it's important how you address the differences. It's a question of emphasis and sensitivity, both of which ultimately come down to how much you know about the different cultures.

"You can only partially pick up the proper sensitivity through seminars. It's extremely helpful if you have had personal experience with different cultures at least once in your life, beyond just traveling."

We asked Kleinfeld to go into detail about some of the finer cultural points he's experienced and how they impact leadership.

Recalling his experience working in Japan, Kleinfeld says, "Always on the first day I came in and we sat together and went over the business issues, and I always assumed that in the evening we'd go out and drink. But I would ask them not to take me to the nice restaurant. I would say, 'Please take me to your favorite bar. And please, let's do a little karaoke singing.' The goal, of course, was to break down the barriers and establish a human relationship. But why it was important was that only by becoming comfortable with one another, by seeing that we had something in common, were we able to then take full advantage of our differences."

We asked Kleinfeld whether he ever had trouble with the pace of decision making in Japan or other cultures, given his drive to make things happen.

"No," he responded, "because you have to set your expectations correctly. So I adjusted my aspiration level and, in addition, I saw that Japanese cultures work a lot with humor, which people usually do not understand. You can actually use a stereotype to make fun of yourself there. And that's what I did again and again. I pushed. If I realized that the push was going too far, I made a joke of myself in a way that everybody laughed about it. They became more comfortable with me, and things came out of that."

Kleinfeld also believes a strong corporate culture is necessary if people from diverse backgrounds are going to work together and produce results. "Again, it comes back to a set of core values and principles that people will all accept as being true. This is more important than it has ever been because we are in an international environment, where the reality is that we are permanently reconfiguring project teams, increasing the number of teams and working in international teams.

"Today, we are solving problems directly in front of customers and throwing people together who have never met each other before. We do not have the luxury people once had—of people together for fiftteen years and getting to know each other.

"Instead, people now come together in one room, and they do not have time to catch up on the fifteen years they missed. They have to start working from the foundation of our common values. When you look at successful organizations, for instance, the Jesuits or the Marines, you find these common values.

"Many people think that a corporate culture means that everybody has to be the same. That is absolutely untrue. Actually, the spice is the diversity. But you need to have the common set of values. Otherwise, things can go overboard and goals can be lost."

For all the attention it requires to manage a diverse workforce, Kleinfeld would not have it any other way. "I very much believe that diversity is a plus," he says. "So much more is accomplished because of it. And it's much more fun. Working hard and having fun are two sides of the same coin. And I also believe that nobody's perfect, but a team can be. I've seen that a hundred times. But only if each member of the team has something unique to offer. If they don't, then the team has the same biases as any one individual, but to a larger degree."

· · ·

The leader who embraces diversity is embracing opportunity. The likelihood of having empathy with customers, clients, and markets is enhanced. The company will be better able to connect with its audiences and build lasting relationships than if it only listened to people who were near identical to one another in their knowledge and perspectives. The recent success of Motorola's cell phone product in both youth and African-American markets is a perfect example of diversity working well.

In the United States and many other markets, young people under the age of twenty-five have become the most highly sought after group by companies selling products that depend on positive word of mouth or "buzz." Unfortunately, this demographic is also the most difficult to reach, since a multitude of stimuli vie for its attention. As a result, companies are appropriating the language and styles with which that generation is most comfortable. To that end, many of them have attached themselves to the hip-hop community.

Marketing experts expect this onetime African-American phenomenon to influence one-quarter of all discretionary spending in America in 2004.[3] By hiring people and bringing in consultants who are comfortable with this language and way of life, companies are making an attempt to capture the attention of young people and a portion of their vast purchasing power.

Motorola, for example, engaged Russell Simmons, founder of the seminal record label Def Jam and considered by many to be the "godfather" of hip-hop, to help with its cell phone product and marketing strategies.

Simmons served as Motorola's channel to an unfamiliar world, one that can often seem vulgar and raw. He steered the company toward the more authentic side of hip-hop, and away from the more squalid.[4] As a result, Motorola has been able to develop an identity that is easier for customers to relate to and has been able to compete in more markets.

Certainly Simmons's point of view was different from then company CEO Christopher Galvin's; his perspective is not what many people might think would come from Motorola. But therein lies the reason for Motorola's growth in previously hard to reach markets. Customers are more willing to see a Motorola phone as hip if it is being endorsed by Russell Simmons. And it is this perceived "hipness" that will increase sales and drive new business opportunities.

According to Harvard Business School professor David Thomas, Motorola is far from the only company that has seen its bottom line benefit as a result of diversity.

"In 1995," Thomas says, "IBM decided a new corporate culture was needed if the company was going to get out of the downward spiral it then found itself in. [Lou] Gerstner [IBM's CEO] made diversity a cornerstone to the transformation. And, at the end of the day, IBM is a stronger company because he did.

"Because the leadership group and the workforce are more diverse, the company has been better at connecting to the diverse marketplace. They've introduced major initiatives to small and medium-sized businesses and done particularly well in companies either owned or managed by women. This has given them a competitive edge. IBM has also done well in its product offerings to the disabled—another competitive edge. Both of these are a direct result of the company's commitment to diversity."

Leaders can embrace diversity, and companies can gain greater business opportunities, not only by having people with contrasting points of view work together, but also by listening to customers. By examining customer buying habits, for example, a company's leadership can gain access to a perspective of which it might not have been previously aware .

Four years after opening its first warehouse in the United States, IKEA was still losing money. Normally, the company realized a profit two or three years after entering a new country. The reason for IKEA's slow acceptance rate in this huge market was cultural.

When entering the United States, IKEA had not seriously considered the possibility that differences existed in this market that made its traditional strategy inappropriate. Unlike many Europeans, for instance, Americans were not patient enough to wait in lines, nor were they liable to understand the metric system of measurement. As a result, they often left IKEA warehouses empty-handed.

To turn IKEA's fortunes around, a number of its fundamental canons had to be changed, beginning with the most basic. No longer could IKEA sell the same product in the same way in one country as it could in another. How the product would be sold in America was still a mystery when Anders Moberg, then IKEA's president and CEO, traveled to U.S. stores in 1989 and 1990.

Recalling the visit, Moberg says, "We were behaving like all Europeans, as exporters, which meant we were not really in the country. It took us time to learn this." [5]

IKEA's products conflicted, sometimes dramatically, with American tastes and even their body types. As reported in an article in the *Economist* in 1994:

> Swedish beds were narrow and measured in centimetres. IKEA did not
> sell the matching bedroom suites that Americans liked. Its kitchen
> cupboards were too narrow for the large dinner plates needed for pizza.
> Its glasses were too small for a nation that piles them high with ice: Mr.
> Carstedt [then head of North American operations] noticed that
> Americans were buying the firm's flower vases as glasses. [6]

In the face of such discrepancies, IKEA's leadership made the decision to adapt. They altered store layout and added new cash registers that increased throughput by some 20 percent. Design changes were made to the furniture to better meet the needs of the U.S. consumer. King- and queen-sized beds, measured in inches, and part of complete suites, were introduced. Bedroom chests were adjusted so that sweaters could better be stored in them.

The company also changed its interpretation of how it could best supply the U.S. market at the lowest cost. No longer were products going to come just from Europe, which made prices vulnerable to currency fluctuations and increased the risk of having too little inventory. To better serve the customers, and to maintain its cherished position as a low-cost leader, management made sure that a large percentage of the furniture sold by IKEA in U.S. stores was produced locally. The results were both dramatic and profound. Sales increased markedly and the turnaround was nearly immediate.

IKEA was made more diverse by paying closer attention to the buying habits of its desired customers. Dissatisfied Americans gave IKEA's leadership insight into points of view that they did not have, widening the management team's perspective on how to best approach the vast U.S. market. The consequences of this more open outlook have been two: first,

IKEA has been able to expand further in the U.S. market and other large markets; second, Anders Moberg and other executives were seen as more capable of fulfilling all that was required of them by their jobs.

This idea of diversity helping an enterprise reach beyond itself is not a new one, nor is it reserved for the world of business. The triumph of the Manhattan Project during World War II, for example, was a direct result of J. Robert Oppenheimer putting together a team of scientists with distinct backgrounds, capable of taking advantage of one another's unique points of view and expertise. The team was tasked by the U.S. government to unlock the mysteries of the atom; this was required if the United States was to develop an atomic weapon before Hitler did. Because the work required unique and dissimilar sets of skills, physicists and chemists had to coexist in order for the project's goals to be met. Further, the unique backgrounds of the major contributors, who hailed from Germany, Italy, Denmark, and the United States, provided a valuable starting point for the team of scientists. Their awareness—especially the Germans'—of what was going on in Europe both facilitated and expedited the work.

No matter where you look, you can find examples of diversity powering innovation, introducing opportunity, and promoting growth. And while many will argue that the Manhattan Project did anything but inspire growth and innovation, we also offer that the work of these scientists opened the atom to the world, thereby bringing forth a scientific breakthrough that has not only proven to be far-reaching but also nothing short of revolutionary.

· · ·

Diversity, we have come to see, is a tool by which a company can gain access to more growth opportunities. It is also a trait that makes organizations more resilient and stronger in times of upheaval.

Proof of this came to us from our conversation with Paul Tagliabue, the commissioner of the National Football League (NFL).

Few leaders have had to face challenges similar to those dealt with by Tagliabue in the days following the 9/11 attacks. While literally breathing the acrid air from the ruins of the World Trade Center, he had to decide whether the NFL would play its games the coming weekend. With so many viewpoints to balance, Tagliabue was under immense scrutiny. Making the situation more troublesome, his decision would also be one of the first public proclamations of how America was going to cope with the tragedy.

In his own words: Paul Tagliabue

"BEFORE MAKING ANY decision, either way, I made a point of listening," Tagliabue says. "There was a lot of consultation. I spoke to a lot of owners, but it was very important to listen to the players and to the public. I spent more time speaking to the head of the players' association than anybody. The players were the ones who were going to have to go out and perform at a time when everyone was finding it hard to function.

"It was particularly hard here in New York and Washington, because some of them had lost friends. Their wives had lost friends. They were as affected as anyone in this area. There were differences of opinion among the players; those in California weren't as affected as those here. Then the players came to the conclusion that they needed a common position."

The players reps voted 17-11 that the games should be called off (two teams were not represented and one abstained). And, in the end, that was what Tagliabue did. "The biggest factor," he says, "was that it was such a shocking, massive loss for the nation to come to grips with."

Some readers may be wondering why we are putting Tagliabue's take on the 9/11 events in this chapter, instead of into those relating to heart and emotional intelligence. The reason is that when the circumstances are such that the normal way of doing things is no longer effective, leaders who do best are generally those used to dealing with a sea of diversity—and Tagliabue is certainly someone who falls into that category.

He is responsible for the security of over a million people who are at NFL stadiums on any given weekend in the autumn. He spends each day balancing the needs of a broad and diverse spectrum of constituencies, including the players, fans, owners, sponsors, and media. As a result, he does something that many leaders do not have to do. He devotes a section of his organization's strategy to "life intruding," which raises the question of how private sector interests and public interests fit together.

While they did not play football in the days following 9/11, Tagliabue says that, if games had been played, the fans' safety concerns would have been met. The implication is that the NFL had already talked to anyone and everyone who may have had something important to say on the subject, conceived of countless worst-case scenarios, and instituted a wide and overlapping range of security measures. Because he has faced the trials inherent in dealing with diverse constituencies, Tagliabue, and by extension the NFL, was more resilient and was better prepared to handle the challenges that appeared immediately after the attacks.

•   •   •

We speak now of how leaders use diversity in order to help their organizations become more resilient. Clearly, the trait is essential to a company's long-term survival. Diversity, however, is important not only to the world of business but also to the world in general.

In the wake of 9/11, many governments became much more focused on the challenge of thwarting terrorists of all sorts, from those trying to blow up buildings to others capable of compromising our infrastructures through technological terrorism. This requires spotting weaknesses before they are exposed, and to do that, governments have increasingly looked to people capable of thoughts that are different than theirs and more in line with the enemy—as the following report from the *Los Angeles Times* illustrates.

> [A San Diego Security firm] used software widely available on the Internet to enter dozens of confidential military and government computers without permission. Among the files they perused: an Army "smart book," detailing radio encryption techniques; hundreds of personnel records containing Social Security numbers, security clearance levels and credit card numbers; and, in one case, "a [Defense Department] memo naming couriers to carry secret documents and their destinations."[7]

When an organization undertakes a challenge like this, it does not rely on middle- or upper-level managers with a wealth of business experience. More likely, they engage a mosaic of people, some perhaps just a few degrees away from being on the wrong side. Others may have little interest in the security process, but instead resonate with the technical challenge. In short, in order to prepare for unorthodox threats, governments have had to marshal a diverse assortment of talents.

The notion of being made resilient by thinking like the enemy is far from new. It is an idea espoused at the highest levels of the government, on the playing field and, of course, in the board room. Its birth, however, most likely came in battle. Military leaders, trying to thwart off a defeat that would most likely end in their death, did all they could to better guarantee their operation's success. To that end, their own actions never monopolized their thougths; instead, contemplating what their enemy would do was what kept them up at night.

FTC commissioner Thomas Leary speaks of this when recalling his days in the Navy:

> (One) lesson goes back to my days in the Navy, before I even went to law school. Shortly after I was commissioned as an Ensign in 1952, I found myself at the Naval Intelligence School in Washington. I learned a lot of fascinating things there, but one experience, in particular, has stuck in my mind ever since. . . .
>
> One of the instructors told us "the role of a good intelligence officer is to act as the enemy's representative on the commander's staff." The *enemy's* representative! Believe me, you sit bolt upright when you hear something like that in wartime. What he meant, of course, was that it was our job to learn as much as we could, from a variety of sources, about the capabilities and the strategies of the enemy—to try to **think like the enemy thinks**—to help the commander anticipate what will happen in battle.[8]

Diversity does indeed make institutions more resilient, but in that resiliency the notion of safety cannot be overlooked. Companies are safer, and their health is better guaranteed as a result of this trait. Look almost anywhere in our world and you can see this same lesson proven again and again. It is dangerous to put all of your eggs in one basket, to put all of your money on one horse.

● ● ●

As we write about diversity, we are aware of many people's preconceptions of what the term represents—equality in the workplace, no matter gender or race. However, the point of this book is to focus on leadership traits that have stood the test of time, and historically, diversity has not been specific to any one minority. So, when talking about what a leader or a company gains by embracing the trait, we have taken a very broad view.

Now, however, as our thoughts shift to the ways in which diversity is best introduced and sustained, we become more focused on what many expect when they think of the word *diversity*.

According to Thomas, in a book he cowrote with John Gabarro titled *Breaking Through: The Making of Minority Executives in Corporate America*, there is no best way to introduce diversity in the workplace. Company type, history, and culture play a large role in determining the best approach, whether it is assimilation, pluralism, or a combination of both.[9] There are, however, conditions that their research has shown to be pivotal if a company's diversity practice is to be successful and sustainable. What follows is a list of those conditions. (Please note that while Thomas and Gabarro's research focuses on people of color, their conclusions apply to any minority group seeking equality in the workplace.)

+ Key executives and senior managers must be involved in and committed to the inclusion of people of color in the organization.

+ If a diversity strategy is to be a success, which is defined by the percentage of minorities in management roles, there must exist a partnership between change-oriented employees and white executives based on a shared commitment to equal opportunity. (There must be present in any organization seeking diversity people who represent the interests of the corporation and those of minorities, men and women who, in their relationships with others, actively pursue the racial diversification of an organization's leadership team.)

+ People of color must be active in promoting change.

+ Diversity must not be limited to the hiring and promotion of people of color. It must also entail minorities' development in core functions of the business and the company's making available to people of color opportunities to enter into management.

+ A company's diversity strategy must be aligned with its culture.[10]

Foremost among the conditions necessary for a sustainable diversity program is the need for top management to support the company's practice.

It is from the top that a tolerant and inclusive environment is created, so that the other conditions listed above can either exist or be effective in promoting equality. By taking an active role in a company's diversity program—by being a mentor, for example—senior management legitimizes the practice, helps remove biases, and improves the quality of work of high-potential candidates.

Without pressure from the top, it is too easy for prejudices or narrow-mindedness to take control. Remaining in one's cultural comfort zone is a dangerous temptation. More often than not, we default to the old adage "Better the devil you know" than chance the risk of the unknown or the different. This is a natural human condition and not easily disrupted.

When leaders are willing to listen to and accept sensibilities that differ from their own, opportunities can be spotted, problems can be avoided, and organizations can be made stronger. Different points of view can serve an organization well, but only if its leaders recognize the value gained by a diverse workforce. It is unfortunate that not all business heads recognize these benefits. Instead of viewing diversity as an asset, they view it as an obligation or, even worse, a liability.

According to Sam Scott—chairman, President and CEO of Corn Products International—the leader who can effectively introduce diversity to a workplace has a particular profile, the most obvious characteristic being his or her understanding of what the word represents, not just what it means.

"There are two types of leaders. The first is that person who is very controlling in management approach, who says that things have to be done in a certain way, often within a specific paradigm.

"The second, and less common, is the leader who examines people, who finds and then accepts their strengths and weaknesses. This person finds immense value in the differences among people, going out of his or her way not only to discover and promote those differences but to make sure that the organization is able to tap into and benefit from whatever makes its employees unique.

"Structure is still in place, but within that structure people are dealt with individually. This is the type of leader who accepts and gains from diversity. He or she is rewarded benefits that the first type of leader, sadly, is not equipped to take hold of.

"And while there are too many leaders of that first type, thankfully, it is not too late in any of their careers to change. People can learn if they're smart enough to realize that there is something to learn. And the first thing that they have to realize is that they already exist in a very diverse arena—the world. Business does not exist in a vacuum. And because it doesn't, what is learned in one place can be applied to another. It takes time and effort, but there are great rewards."

John A. Luke Jr., chairman and CEO of the MeadWestvaco, is a person whom we qualify as someone who actively promotes and seeks out fresh and different perspectives. His take on diversity is a personal one, the result of it having evolved into a leading role in his career's development.

"Luke told us, "What helped me grow and move along this leadership journey has been my decision to open myself up to many of different types of people. This has meant being actively engaged in the business and expecting more from other leaders. Because of this, I think I've been better able to respond to the series of changes that the company and the industry have undergone."

Luke admits that this approach is very much a skill he has had to cultivate. "I would like to say that I have always been open to different perspectives, but, in truth, it took me time to recognize that being too directive meant I wasn't letting in the people I wanted to hear from."

Being open to a diverse range of perspectives requires a willingness to suspend judgment for a period of time, and to resist the temptation of falling back on what one is most comfortable with.

Luke points out, "While, in most cases, I walk into a situation with a pretty good idea of where I would like to see things go, I want to have some of my own thinking tested and developed by the contribution of those with different perspectives. When you do that, there really is a much greater chance to create an even better idea."

Many of our interviews focused on the topics of effectively introducing diversity to the workplace and who is most capable of managing a diverse workforce. In fact, these two very important issues could well serve as the topic of a book. We believe that Harvard University's David Thomas has provided us with the most eloquent perspective on these topics.

In his own words: David Thomas

THE TYPE OF PERSON who most effectively introduces and manages a diverse workforce is the one who realizes that everyone is diverse. Diversity does not refer only to ethnic minorities; it can encompass thought, gender, sexual orientation, physical disability—the list is a long one. Because it's so long, diversity cannot be avoided. It is the reality to any workplace. The leader who understands this is someone also who understands that the way you manage diversity is to create an inclusive environment.

"Diversity is cosmetic. It is what the people from the outside see when they look in. Inclusion, which is an environment that must be created, is really what we are referring to when we talk about being diverse. A company can have diverse workforce, but if people don't feel that they are included or valued, what problems are being solved?

"As a leader, if you're going to be effective, you need to think about how you're going to create that environment in which everyone feels included. To do that, you need to create an environment where everyone feels that his or her uniqueness is valued, no matter whether the differences concern sexual orientation, race, or gender.

"Now, having this mindset is just the starting-off point. A leader is not fully embracing diversity without taking two more steps. First, he or she needs to create an environment that is developmental in addition to being inclusive. People need to feel that, as a result of engaging with others who are different than they are, they are being given an opportunity to develop and that they are developing.

"Second, the leader must always be willing to learn from people's differences. Because people are different, they will have different perspectives about work; about how the company could better serve its clients and customers; about where there are opportunities; about the ways in which the company's current operating processes advantage or disadvantage people. Leaders have to constantly be in the mode of learning from those differences, so that if they are approached with a suggestion about how to do something better, the conversation will be informative and constructive.

"This type of person should be successful at bringing diversity into a company and managing a diverse workforce, because they provide alternatives to what, most likely, had existed before. By listening to and learning from people who were historically excluded, that's not only empowering but it's also enabling. From this process, from this type of manager, minorities see an alternative route to success, something far different that what, most likely, had existed before.

Three barriers have long existed that have hindered minorities' advancement in the workplace. First is prejudice. The negative biases people have toward members of different groups have forced minorities to fight against the notion that they are somehow inferior. With each new position, minorities have to establish their standing and challenge stereotypes. A consequence can be that some minority employees internalize prejudices. They lower their own expectations, creating further obstacles for their own advancement.

Second, minorities have been disadvantaged as a result of issues relating to comfort and risk. Because dominant group members are often uncomfortable mixing with their minority peers, the latter are often excluded from social networks and are less likely to gain the support of others, which is necessary to advance. In addition, members of the majority are hesitant to sponsor minority protégés, believing that doing so puts them at greater risk, because greater scrutiny historically applied to those who supported minorities instead of traditional candidates. As a result, Thomas and Gabarro point out, minorities are often not positioned to take on the high-profile job assignments that will get them noticed and facilitate promotion.

Third, the ability for minorities to advance in a business environment has historically been handicapped by the fact that few companies had the capabilities to effectively identify high-potential minority candidates. But given the existence of prejudices and the issues of discomfort, this should not be seen as a surprise.[11]

It is from this context of injustice that many corporate diversity programs were first born. In some instances it was because of government regulation, but in most it was a sense of morality that led many business leaders and companies to create a fairer playing field. They did this, and are still doing this, by focusing on three principles: creating an enabling organizational environment, ensuring that opportunity exists, and ensuring that development takes place.[12] These principles, as mentioned earlier, are articulated in different ways, depending on a variety of factors, the foremost being a company's culture.

At Corn Products International, for example, Scott, who is an African-American, has focused on creating an environment that not only values variation but also asks for people to better understand one another's differences and to accept them; a place where people are given both the opportunity learn and to practice what they have learned. Scott endorses inclusion and he works hard to insure that people of difference are never at a disadvantage.

Such a focus has been effective, and without a doubt, improvements have been made. But new challenges have been presented to leaders and their companies. As a result, the way companies have approached equality in the workplace has changed; the drivers of diversity have to find support for diversity programs to remain effective.

Explains Thomas, "The differences between today and the 1970s and '80s, when many diversity programs really took root—especially in the United States—is that then we were in the midst of a societal movement toward a more equitable society. This made it easier to create momentum around the idea of diversity in the workplace.

"Today, the debate tends to center on whether the differences we see in opportunities are the result of the system remaining inequitable or a function of deficiencies of those people in minority groups.

"For example, consider the conversations about women in today's workplace. The argument can be made that companies have done everything that they could, that they made available opportunities, but for some reason or another, women don't want to take them. They prefer to have a family or to do something on their own. To that, however, I would argue that compromises are still being made, and companies remain inflexible, albeit in different ways. In the past, it was about opportunity. Now it has to also include how that opportunity is being presented.

"Women are making the choices they make because what alternatives do they have? To live like a man? Because that's the choice many big businesses have given them. To succeed, to take advantage of certain opportunities, women have to behave and, on some level, live in a certain way. Unfortunately, that way is not very comfortable to them. In fact, it's very male and not in line with how they imagine themselves to be. And what's worse, if they adapt, if they apply this male template to themselves so that they can succeed, then they're often seen as being less than a woman and often a bitch."

Diversity programs have to adapt. Leaders must realize that to be seen as effective and continue to gain benefits from the notion of diversity, it is not enough to do what they have always done. The measures taken in the past are not always going to be effective for every situation, nor are the challenges a company faces regarding equality always going to remain the same.

Thomas talks of this last point when he tells us that much of what business leaders are focusing on now, when it comes to diversity, has to do with the level of minority representation in executive ranks. He says, "Many executives feel embarrassed by the lack of people of color in corner offices.

"Although the system has changed and although it may be operating more judiciously, it is still not fixed. It is the system itself that continues to produce the inequality at the highest levels of a corporation. That's where the moral concern now lies, and where diversity campaigns and business leaders are placing their focus.

"The next generation of minority high potentials is probably not going to be as patient as the last one, especially now that more minorities have the same educational background and problem-solving skills as their majority peers. They are less likely to wait for the right opportunity to present itself. If companies continue in the same pattern, it is likely that there will be even less diversity at the tops of organizations than there is now."

Minorities have been viewed for too long as not having essential leadership traits and have not been given equal access to executive opportunities. Many business leaders, through their companies' diversity programs, are trying to refute this notion.

Pattie Dunn, former global chief executive of Barclays Global Investors, believes trust is essential if a diversity program is going to be successful in today's corporate environment. Too often minorities are discriminated against as a result of the majority overstating what is different about them and declaring that those difference are wrong. Says Dunn, "If people just talk to one other—assuming that they feel safe enough to tell each other what they really think—they'd realize that there are so many more things they have in common than not." As an executive, Dunn opines, sometimes it necessary to use the commonalities to overcome biases. The result, she says, is that people have more reason to trust others and not turn their backs on one another.

Dunn is realistic about the challenges relating to the process of building trust among disparate groups, but she is also certain of rewards. She explains, "As people begin to trust one another, they become capable of working more effectively. And when that happens, there is far less tension in the workplace and far more cooperation, and progress can be made, meaning there will be more and more minorities in important positions."

For Dunn and others, the power of diversity is most effectively harnessed in today's marketplace through meritocracies. Speaking at one time to an interviewer she said, "In a meritocracy, you will see much more . . . balance. My message to [minorities] is, if you're not working for [a meritocrat], move on."[13]

The leadership traits discussed in this book have been demonstrated by and apply to all types of human beings. The ability to be an effective leader is not defined by the color of skin, sexual orientation, or gender. It is defined, instead, by qualities to which others, can connect, traits that make no mention of physical appearance.

As noble a thought that this is, we do not live or work in a world without biases. While it is true that the qualities of leadership know no color or gender, it is equally true that the minorities who have reached the tops of their organizations have done so by placing more faith in some traits than in others. We think it is worth mentioning that emotional intelligence is what many believe to be most essential for minorities' advancement.

Says Thomas, "Emotional intelligence is so important because it is about two things: first, self-awareness, which is the knowledge of who you are and the impact you have on others; second, self-regulation or the ability to take in what's going on in your environment but prevent it from such influence that it sways you from doing what is right. Given the circumstances of many minorities, in order to succeed, the most necessary skills are to channel their anger, be empathetic toward others, and advocate their views without people thinking that they are arbitrary or punitive."

● ● ●

The fact that we are not all the same is something to celebrate; it is what makes life interesting and so full of possibilities. No matter how open each of us is to these differences, there is always room—and reason—for us to broaden our perspective. That is the message of this chapter, and in many ways the message of this entire book. An individual—or a business—is never so successful that adjustments cannot be made to improve performance.

In this interconnected, interdependent world of ours, narrow-mindedness, prejudice, and cultural ignorance are increasingly dangerous. Survival demands that our leaders have the ability to subjugate their egos and prejudices for the greater good of the organization and community. Corporate leadership, however, does not begin and end with the decisions being made by the chief executive officer. Because of this, we close our discussion with a few words on diversity as it relates to boards of directors.

Historically, boards were comprised of the friends and advisors of the founder or CEO of a company. Board members were usually of the same age and peer group as this executive officer. As corporate leadership was most often white and male, so, too, were the board members. The boardroom was a club. The number of members was determined by the whims of the lead officer and the complexity and size of the business.

With the recent focus on issues related to governance, much has changed in the boardroom. As a result of such regulations as Sarbanes-Oxley attention is now on the relationship between members of the board and a company's leadership team; board member independence has become increasingly important as has boardroom diversity.

We thought that these new regulations and the increased attention on issues related to diversity would have resulted in more women and minorities rising to board positions. With CEOs now declining to sit on more than two or three boards, corporations must look at a larger pool of candidates, which has resulted in women and minorities becoming key targets. Yet we must ask why white males still maintain the majority of board seats?

Boardroom diversity is increasing proportionately with the number of women and minorities in the executive ranks of large companies. When more women and minorities accelerate through the ranks of academic institutions and corporations, and become successful, we will begin to see them make gains in the boardroom as well. One success leads to another, so in order to address the issue of boardroom diversity, we must first address the issue of whether corporate culture has embraced the need to augment the ranks of its institutions with women and minorities, thus positioning them as prime candidates for board positions.

While the trend of growth at corporations and institutions for women and minorities is slow, the momentum and drive for them to enter the boardroom will increase over the next five years. While we are pleased that the trend is occurring, we are disappointed that it is taking longer than we had hoped. Nevertheless, we are encouraged by the growth, and there is more excitement throughout America today in pushing for diversity than we saw anytime in the 1990s.

The 1990s brought us a focus on the Internet. Instead of diversity, youth and dot-com candidates became a board profile in the late 1990s. Today, diversity and wisdom have become the dominant theme of boardroom corporate governance. We are also beginning to see that corporate boards are looking for the best candidates as opposed to looking at candidates that fit into any one category, such as diversity or women. It is a beginning, the start of a trend, and it is the start of what we believe will result in greater diversity in the boardroom five years from now.

•   •   •

No matter what level in the organization, diversity is now—and will become increasingly so—a key element in building winning teams and strategies. As more companies realize how small the world is, and how expansive their reach can be, they will come to see more clearly the imperative of having a dynamic, multiopinioned, multicultured workforce.

In this chapter, we have shown that diversity can lead to more market opportunities and make a company more resilient in the face of known and unknown challenges. Yes, a diverse workforce is good for business. But the advantages of being inclusive and valuing a multitude of perspectives go well beyond the obvious bottom-line components.

We started this book with the notion that true leaders are those who do not want to live "a little life." Now, wanting to live a "big life" without certain values and ethical standards can indeed bring about undesirable results. So, it is more than just wanting to live a big life. We talked about people who wanted their actions to make the world a better place, in some meaningful way, regardless of the size of the community impacted.

In many ways, successfully creating an integrated, diverse workforce at all levels accomplishes that mission. Whether it is the sum of the parts being greater than the whole, or the learning that each individual achieves from exposure to different ideas and perceptions, or the sense of empowerment groups of people achieve that in turn enables them to empower subsequent generations or communities—diversity brings about a higher quality of participation and existence.

In between the first and last chapters, we have covered powerful traits that leaders utilize to accomplish their mission. For the individual reader, we have not offered a guaranteed formula, as we recognize that each individual and situation is unique. However, each reader can recognize elements of himself or herself throughout the book and, we believe, work to leverage their natural leadership traits along with the commitment to live a life that makes the world a better place. While that may seem a bit clichéd for the conclusion of a business book, it is indeed the formula we suggest. Drive and commitment, coupled with humility and empathy and respect for others, produce the most solid foundation possible on which to build leadership that endures.

A perspective from the Russell Reynolds Associates Executive Assessment Team

Leadership exists in the eyes and perceptions of followers. Without followers, leadership by definition could not exist. No matter the leadership traits an individual possesses, he or she cannot be successful without assembling and motivating a team to carry out his or her vision. To do this effectively, it is imperative that leaders attract and develop a diverse group of individuals for their team and be able to appeal to individuals with varied personalities, cultures, professional backgrounds, and work styles.

In building a diverse team, it is important to select individuals who share the organization's values, but offer a diversity of skills and approaches to achieve the organization's goals. Thus, a leader who seeks to find team members who share his or her training, experiences, and thinking style may later find himself or herself, as well as the organization, stagnant and unable to grow or creatively solve problems. Rather, by selecting a team of individuals who can approach a problem or a strategic dilemma from varying perspectives, a team will benefit from a variety of innovative ideas as well as having a productive dialogue

sources

1. Selected quote, "Diversity," http://learningtogive.org/search/quotes/ Display_Quotes.asp?page_num=2&subject_id=60&search_type=subject (accessed April 19, 2004).
2. Selected quote, "Diversity," http://www.ifla.org/faife/litter/subject/pluralism.htm (accessed March 8, 2004).
3. Susan Berfield, with Diane Brady and Tom Lowry, "The CEO of Hip Hop," *Business Week*, October 27, 2003.
4. Ibid.
5. Management Brief, *Economist*, November 19, 1994.
6. Ibid.
7. Janet Reitman, "Cyberdudes to the Rescue," *Los Angeles Times Magazine*, November 17, 2002.
8. Thomas Leary, "Lessons from True Life: True Stories That Illustrate the Art and Science of Cost-Effective Counseling," *Antitrust Source* 2, no. 4 (March 2003), http://www.ftc.gov/speeches/leary/a59learynew319.pdf (accessed February 22, 2004).
9. According to Thomas and Gabarro, assimilation proposes that discriminating behavior can best be eradicated by making race and ethnicity less visible. Pluralism, in contrast, maintains that racial and ethnic identity not be abandoned in a company's drive to integrate. Pluralism is founded on the ideology that an organization is made better by the presence of different identities.
10. Thomas and Gabarro, *Breaking Through*, p. 189.
11. Ibid., pp. 26–29.
12. Ibid, p. 214.
13. Christopher Springman, "Dunn Deals: Interview with Patricia Dunn," *Chief Executive*, July 2001.